NEW FEDERAL POLICIES FOR R&D

Impacts on Government, Industry & Academe

Proceedings of the Thirty-Eighth National Conference on The Advancement of Research

Edited by

Nanette S. Levinson
College of Public and International Affairs
The American University

UNIVERSITY
PRESS OF
AMERICA

LANHAM • NEW YORK • LONDON

All University Press of America books are produced on acid-free
paper which exceeds the minimum standards set by the National
Historical Publications and Records Commission.

PREFACE

The thirty-eighth National Conference On The Advancement of Research (NCAR) was held on October 7 - 10, 1984 in Williamsburg, Virginia. Hosted by the College of Public and International Affairs of The American University, Washington, D.C., this conference brought together leaders from the public, private, university and not-for-profit sectors.

This book reflects the expert work of Thomas Hogan of the National Science Foundation and his program committee in crafting a program which identified and assessed the impacts of R&D policy during the Reagan administration. The chapters of this book set forth administration, industry, university, and not-for-profit perspectives. Each perspective is followed by a discussion with questions and comments from participants.

I would like to acknowledge the contributions of numerous individuals in making this conference successful and this book a reality. My NCAR colleagues including Gen. A.W. Betts, Southwest Research Institute, and Dr. Norman Waks, the MITRE Corporation, provided advice and inspiration. Dr. Robert E. Cleary, Dean of the College of Public and International Affairs, graciously offered the support of his office for conference administration. Ms. Judith Sidor provided key assistance at all stages of the conference. Mr. Terry Lockhart was a superb conference coordinator. He was ably assisted by Ms. Nadine Granoff and Ms. Margy Hoppin of the Center for Technology and Administration. Finally and importantly, Mr. Michael Murphy handled the word processing and formatting of this book, moving with ease from transcript to final copy.

Nanette S. Levinson
The American University
Washington, D.C.

TABLE OF CONTENTS

Preface
Program Committee
Conference Committee
Overview

NATIONAL CONFERENCE ON THE ADVANCEMENT OF RESEARCH

EXECUTIVE SECRETARY

N. Waks

CONFERENCE COMMITTEE

A. W. Betts, Chair
D. W. Barnes, Chair-Elect
C. B. Amthor
R. C. Anderson
D. L. Baeder
G. L. Bata
C. L. Chernick
E. G. L. Cilley
C. J. Cook
M. J. Cooper
T. J. Hogan
G. R. Holcomb
J. Holmfeld
S. A. Johnson, Jr.
D. N. Langenberg
C. F. Larson
N. S. Levinson
J. Lewallen
J.C. McKee
E. Milbergs
H. G. Pfeiffer
C. Pings
D. Prager
W. R. Richard
C. M. Schoman, Jr.
S. M. Tennant
N. Waks
J. J. B. Worth
L. Young

PROGRAM COMMITTEE

OVERVIEW

Nanette S. Levinson
The American University

Examining the impacts of recent R&D policies yields a vivid yet kaleidoscopic view of R&D processes in our national context. Not only do R&D policies impact industry, university and not-for-profit organizations; these organizations themselves can impact R&D policies. Perspectives on these impacts are rooted in the sector from which one comes. Each sector has its own values, culture and concerns.

The papers in this volume reflect these perspectives and concerns. Taken together they constitute a unique panorama-- a comprehensive and considered glimpse of inputs to the R&D process (funding, facilities and personnel), policies relating to the R&D process and outputs of the process both in the short and long term. These papers and discussions identify direct and indirect impacts. Of particular note are impacts on those factors which facilitate or hinder the R&D process and on those groups involved in the process. Finally, the papers highlight a key characteristic of recent R&D policy, the changing interrelationships of these groups.

Charles Falk's paper provides a quantitative foundation for discussing U.S. R&D processes. He focuses on R&D expenditures as inputs to the R&D process. Broadening this focus, Albert Teich's paper examines the sociopolitical context for R&D. He highlights three elements: the changing perceptions and attitudes toward national security, the increasingly important national and international economic situation, and the changing perceptions and attitudes toward the role of government in society.

As John Holmfeld remarks in his introductory comments, science has now entered the "big leagues." Christopher Hill's paper provides solid evidence of this transition. He discusses the Congressional role in R&D policy and examines the increasing number of bills before Congress.

Providing additional evidence of attention to R&D policy, James Ling's paper supplies the philosophy behind the R&D statistics from an executive branch perspective. Ling's paper ties in the discussion of R&D expenditures to a "revitalized economy. . ., restored defense posture," and R&D accomplishments.

Within this complex context of executive and congressional branch initiatives, Ian Ross in his keynote paper points out a realignment among the players involved in R&D. This realignment is reflected in industry's increased funding of R&D and increased focus on the leading edge. The paper by Mary Good discusses in further detail this "surging vitality of the nation's industrial laboratories." She clearly identifies the laboratories' roles and linkages to other performers in the R&D process. As a part of the discussion of linkages, she argues for the R&D tax credit.

Milton Stewart highlights a key role in this "surging vitality," the role of small business. His paper is a candid portrayal of the significant contributions of small business to U.S. innovation. It also discusses the strong impacts of R&D policy elements upon small business and upon their interrelationships with other R&D performers. While Milton Stewart sets forth the spirit and philosophy of small business, Samuel Tinsley provides a discussion of the philosophy of large industry. His paper calls for an examination of policies other than those items traditionally included in the term R&D policies. In particular he identifies regulatory-type policies which impact industrial R&D.

There are three papers which provide university viewpoints on R&D policies and their impacts. Robert Barker's paper discusses R&D issues from the perspective of a university provost. His paper raises issues of central concern to the university community including indirect costs and scientific communication and national security. It also examines the role of state governments in promoting R&D. The vitality of this role can also clearly be seen in Governor Charles Robb's remarks on R&D activity in the Commonwealth of Virginia.

From the perspective of a university scientist, William Risen's paper vividly portrays the concerns, pressures and needs of today's faculty researcher. Particular attention is paid to the demands of frequent proposal writing, the presence of inadequate and aging equipment, and the problems of a separate funding organization for engineering research.

Calling for a longer term view in the discussion of R&D impacts, the Donald Langenberg paper written from a chancellor's perspective reminds us of the unique characteristics of academe. It also emphasizes the importance of the education function of universities and the role of this education function and related policies in contributing to U.S. productivity.

The range of subjects and perspectives covered in these papers as a whole reflects the complexity and creativity inherent in R&D processes themselves. This range is also evident in George Gamota's useful report on the small group discussions and Charles Schoman's cogent synthesis of the entire proceedings.

CHAPTER ONE
Introduction

General A. W. Betts
Southwest Research Institute

Good morning, and welcome to the 38th Annual Conference on the Advancement of Research, NCAR-38, as we familiarly refer to it. I am currently Consultant to the President of Southwest Research Institute in San Antonio.

As chairman, I declare these proceedings to be open and I think we should get on with what brought us to Williamsburg.

This gavel, complete with the names of those who have chaired this meeting before me, is NCAR's only tangible asset unless you call address lists tangible assets.

We especially treasure this gavel because it reminds us of our origins in Penn State back in 1947, and I just as soon leave it at that point.

I wish that all of you could see the comments on each of these speakers because they are very interesting. For example, Don Baeder, the year he was chairman, drew the title Baeder's Boisterous Belittler, which fits.

I'm not quite sure what was meant when they put me down here as Betts Blooming Boomer, but I leave it to your fun.

Those of you who were here last year or those of you who read the promotional material for this year's meeting will recall NCAR-38 is the second of two annual meetings during which we will focus on our national R&D policies as they have evolved over the life of the current administration.

We seek to generate a discussion that will inform you about these policies and explore their impact on the four sectors that make up NCAR; that is, government, industry, academia and the independent R&D organizations that we inaccurately, but familiarly, refer to as the not-for-profits.

Last year we considered the nature of the changes of policy that have been made or surely were in contemplation at that time.

This year we will expand on that discussion of changes in policy and explore as best we can the impacts of those changes on the four mentioned sectors.

The final objective, of course, is to develop informed views on just how we, as managers of R&D from the four sectors, should adjust to the changes. But enough about program. You will hear more of that from Tom Hogan as Chairman of the Program Committee.

For now I want to inform those who are new and remind those who have been with us before that we want very much to encourage discussion among you, both at the sessions and during those nonmeeting times that you will have together.

The whole purpose of NCAR is to foster effective interaction among representatives of the four sectors for the greater good of all. That basic theme is what is behind making this an invitational meeting, not that we seek an elite group as such, but rather as a pragmatic approach to encouraging informal and free discussions.

As has been our custom, all of the talks and the question and answer periods will be recorded and published in the proceedings.

Since NCAR has no permanent organizational structure except for our esteemed Executive Secretary, Norm Waks, we rely on members of the Conference Committee to carry the burden of those activities that keep NCAR alive and result in annual meetings such as this one.

I would like to have you meet some of those people. First I would ask Norm Waks to stand so that you may identify him. Thank you, our Executive Secretary, Chief Management Scientist for the Mitre Corporation.

Next, at that table in front of you is Tom Hogan, Study Director, Industry Studies, of the National Science Foundation and Program Chairman, whose committee will bring us at this meeting an outstanding group of speakers.

And then I would like to introduce Nanette Levinson, the Director, Advanced Technology Management Program, of The American University, who is the host representative responsible for all the planning and the excellent arrangements that go so far to make for a successful meeting.

And looking ahead I would like to introduce Jay Lewallen, Vice-president of Southwest Research Institute, who is Program Chairman for NCAR-39. That will be held in Keystone, Colorado, next year.

And while we are on that subject, let me introduce Sandy Johnson, Director of Denver Research Institute, who will be our host for this meeting in Keystone.

Beyond Keystone is NCAR-40. That will be a joint meeting with

2

the Canadian Research Management Association, to be held in the Chateau Frontenac in Quebec City, Canada, in September of 1986. Tom Hogan for NCAR and George Bota for CRNA will jointly chair that meeting.

Now to get on with the meeting. I want to ask Nanette Levinson, as Conference Host, if she will introduce our welcoming speaker. Nanette.

NANETTE LEVINSON
The American University

Thank you, Cy. I would like to share with you one of my favorite sayings. It comes from Will Rogers. Will Rogers once said, "When you don't know where you're going there are many ways of getting there."

This morning I have the pleasure of introducing to you an individual who not only provides leadership in identifying where we are going, but in a clear-cut, effective and efficient manner gets us at our university and, in fact, in the higher education community, to where we are going.

This individual, our President, Dr. Richard Berendzen, has energized our faculty, our students, our alumni and the entire university community. He has led us to meet our objectives in a very efficient and effective fashion.

Dr. Berendzen received his undergraduate degree from the Massachusetts Institute of Technology and master's and doctoral degrees from Harvard University.

He will not only officially welcome you this morning, but will share with you some of the broad vision and great energy which we see on our campus and which will initiate the program for this thirty-eighth annual meeting. Dr. Berendzen.

DR. RICHARD BERENDZEN
The American University

Thank you, Nanette. Many of you are from other universities, and I know you have been enjoying Williamsburg and have been commenting about the waterfall and the trees. You are aware, of course, that this is simply an extended part of the campus of American University. I wish that it were so.

I wonder about an organization that seems as subversive as this. If word gets out, we are all in trouble -- no dues and, until recently, no executive secretary. That is not the American way. How can you run research institutions like that?

We are proud to be associated with you; we are proud to be the host institution. I am also proud of another historical first for your organization. You just heard from the young woman who has been the organizer. I gather that this is the first time a woman has had this post in your organization. I commend you for this progress and am proud The American University is associated with it.

In the entrance area there are brochures about our university. One of them refers to 50 years of service in public sector education. In fact, the university is 91 years old; we have been involved in public administration education for a half century.

Washington, D.C., provides us with unique opportunities, and not only in R&D but also in the study of law, government, economics, and a host of other fields. We hope that if you have not done so in the past, you will take the opportunity to visit the university in Washington. Then feel that it is your second alma mater.

There is another part of your mission in this meeting, which I am sure you will undertake and I wish you well on it. The nation desperately has needed a revival in its independent R&D activity. You know that well. There has been some recent progress, but not nearly enough and the activities in which you are engaged are intimately linked with other cardinal concerns in our society.

While many of you are not in educational institutions -- you work in the private sector, government or elsewhere -- those of you who are in universities know the pain through which our nation has gone the last year and a half. Those of you who have hired graduates during the last ten to fifteen years know that the clarion call was correct in April of 1983, when a vital report came out. It was a thin book, a very small one. In fact, advisors on that book said, "Don't make it longer or it will exceed the attention span of the American public." The title of

5

the book could not have been more simple, A Nation at Risk.

It told the stunning story of how our country dropped in its intellectual, academic and educational skills and performance. In no area was that drop worse than in math and science. In fact, during the last fifteen years in international comparison tests our students placed first not a single time and placed last many times.

What we need are closer partnerships and bonds. We should have known that all along. Employers told educators that the graduates they were hiring simply were not well prepared. The university people knew it but somehow could not communicate it to the high schools. The parents intuited it but did nothing about it. The news media should have known it but did not report to it. In short, we long have needed a caring, responsive partnership. Today, however, we stand a good chance of rectifying that.

In so far as there has been a drop of student interest in engineering and high-tech fields, this has reflected a general national ethos. There was another staggering fact, too, only a few years ago, more than half of all graduate students in the U.S. in engineering were from foreign countries. That in itself was sobering, but what made it even more jolting was the realization that the foreign students were better than the American ones. Something went awry when we found students from Korea and Taiwan, Hong Kong, and elsewhere academically ahead of U.S. students.

Well, your responsibilities lie with research, not education, but they are not disassociated from one another. During the decade of the seventies, the U.S. produced more lawyers than any other time in our society. At the same time, we produced fewer and fewer scientists and engineers. Lawyers are important; in so far as greater numbers of them contribute to social injustice, I am for it. But, engineers exist to create; lawyers do to litigate.

One of the reasons I am pleased that The American University -- through Nanette Levinson -- has been involved with this imporant organization that I know you deal with the creation of knowledge and benefit of our society.

Again, on behalf of The American University I want to welcome you. If there is any way we can assist you, we would like to do so ... not only during this conference, but in the future.

Welcome to YOUR conference.

6

Dr. Dennis Barnes
University of Virginia

DR. BETTS: We took advantage of the fact that Dennis Barnes, after he left the Washington scene, came to Virginia and assumed a research role in the University of Virginia.

DR. BARNES: This is the preliminary or unofficial welcome on behalf of the Commonwealth. The Governor of Virginia, Chuck Robb, had wanted to be here. He could not make it in his schedule today. The Governor will be meeting us tomorrow at 12:15 in this room.

This is the 14th size state in population. It is probably the largest in sense of tradition or heritage, so much so some folks would say that we look at Williamsburg as the city of tomorrow. But it is a state not normally associated with the sorts of things we will be talking about today.

It is the headquarters of two of the largest railroads in the country, N&W and CSX. It has a major ship building facility down in Newport News. Tobacco is a big agricultural product. None of these are the sorts of things we would say are on the cutting edge.

Less familiar to people is that these also contain one of the highest concentrations of high-technology industry. Northern Virginia alone is one of the centers of telecommunications in the country, with over 850 high-technology companies. In the Small Business Innovation Research Program that the government conducts, Virginia is third following Massachusetts and California. Those are the less familiar sides of Virginia.

I would have to point out that Virginia has taken the lead in trying to organize a number of the southern states, 32 academic institutions in the southeast, to build this country's next generation or one of the next major electron accelerators in the country and if we are successful this will be because of a design that originated at one of the universities in the southeast, the University of Virginia. It went out in competition against national laboratories across the country.

There is one other current innovation in Virginia that I will leave to the governor to talk about tomorrow, and that is the Center for Innovative Technology, about which you may have noted items in the New York Times and the Wall Street Journal.

It is exciting and very untypical sort of innovation for Virginia. This is the Governor's doing and I will not detract

7

from that. With those brief remarks, I would like to pass the gavel on to Tom Hogan, your Program Chairman.

DR. HOGAN: First I would like to take a few minutes to tell you a little bit more about the program for the next three days. Cy has already given you a general view of it, but let me go into a little bit more detail.

As most of you know, this is the second part of a two-conference review on the impacts of government science and technology policy, both that of the administration and of the Congress, on the various sectors of the economy.

The importance of this topic and the broad ramifications that it has for future US economic growth led us to the decision to devote both last year's conference at San Antonio, as well as this one, to the same subject area.

A year ago our primary focus was on obtaining a better understanding of the government policies and practices that had been put into effect up to that point.

We also tried to obtain some preliminary input regarding the impacts at the third-year level point in the administration.

Our emphasis this year will be somewhat different in that we will focus more heavily on these perceived impacts and less on an explanation of what it has all been about.

We thought that this seemed to be a particularly appropriate time to do this in as much as election day is only a month away.

In putting the program together, our committee purposely tried to attract a wide variety of speakers representing people from many diverse organizations. I hope we have been successful.

To reiterate what Cy Betts said earlier, one of the thrusts that NCAR has always tried to accomplish is to encourage as much audience participation as possible. Similarly we have provided many opportunities for you to mingle with our speakers, as well as the other attendees during the course of this conference.

I particularly want to mention and emphasize the small group session scheduled for the second half of tomorrow morning. This will afford you a particularly tangible opportunity to make sure that your views with regard to these federal policies and their impacts are heard and incorporated in our overall summary. Also each session moderator has made a point of setting aside sufficient time to allow you to ask a number of questions of the speakers.

I would like to turn now to the keynote address. Our keynote speaker this year is Dr. Ian Ross, the President of AT&T-Bell Laboratories, a position he has held since April of 1979. Dr. Ross was trained as an electrical engineer, receiving both his graduate and undergraduate degrees from Cambridge University.

In addition to being responsible for running one of the most important research facilities in the world, Dr. Ross is also involved in numerous outside activities. For example, he serves as a member of several corporate boards of directors. He has received numerous awards for both his professional and private achievement.

He is also a member both of the National Academy of Sciences and the National Academy of Engineering. It is indeed a real pleasure to introduce our keynote speaker, Dr. Ian Ross.

CHAPTER TWO
KEYNOTE ADDRESS
"R&D for Industrial Competitiveness"

Ian Ross
AT&T - Bell Laboratories

I was delighted to accept this invitation to speak here, an invitation you sent out many months ago. I was horrified to learn about four weeks ago that I had to attend an important AT&T conference that starts at noon today. The bad news, as far as I am concerned, is it means I can't remain with you at this conference. The good news is, by colossal coincidence, it happens to be held in Williamsburg just across the street.

At breakfast this morning I mentioned to one of my AT&T colleagues that I would be talking here. He said, "Isn't that interesting. Tens years ago I talked in that very auditorium." He said it was the first time he had ever worn bifocals. And when he finished his talk he stepped off the elevated podium, fell flat on his face, and he got the best round of applause he had ever gotten. So, I am relieved to see I am at ground level and you people are above.

Clearly this conference brings together an imporant combination of people and subjects at a very critical time. The people, of course, are those of universities, industry and government. The subject is R&D. And it is a time when almost everyone recognizes the extent to which our economy and our social success depend upon our R&D leadership and its relationship to industrial competitiveness. That is what I want to talk about.

Incidentally, one of the pleasant experiences I am having is working on the President's Commission on Industrial Competetiveness, and I will talk about that just a little bit.

Now, much has already been written on this general subject, and I will mention later some of the conventional wisdom. But I would like to go beyond these and focus upon an important industrial thrust, "a synergy of sectors" you might call it, a bringing together of the strengths of our universities, our industry and our government to provide a contribution to our total effectiveness for the nation.

I think this is right on target with some of the themes expressed in your program for this year, which includes the words "How each R&D-performing sector of the economy -- government, industry, universities, and other nonprofit institutions -- can best play its vital and unique role, while simultaneously interacting to strengthen the overall infrastructure of our country." Very, very, important to all!

Let me begin by ignoring Satchel Paige's oft-quoted advice. He said, "Don't look back -- someone might be gaining on you!" Well, someone is gaining on us. But we also know that our past and current strengths and capabilities are very great. The important thing, though, is to assess these capabilities correctly and use them to our advantage.

In the past our strengths were overwhelmingly clear: We had abundant resources, excellent education, sound infrastructure. We had a large and, at times, growing domestic market. Much of this remains. Much is being revitalized today because we have been jolted by the concept that "someone is gaining on us." And we do have to build, and build on, these basic strengths. But I think we also have to develop new strengths and new approaches in line with these new challenges.

This is particularly true in the case of our R&D and its relationship to industrial competitiveness. In that regard I think it is all too easy, still, to look only at the aggregate figures on R&D in this country and remain complacent.

For example, if you look at the total R&D budget, which you know in 1984 is approaching $100 billion (97.9 billion), that is an 11 percent increase over the previous year -- which is good. That $100 billion exceeds the combined total R&D budgets of our major industrial competitors; namely Britain, France, West Germany and Japan. Even in terms of percentage of gross national product, our 2.7 percent exceeds all but West Germany's 2.8 percent.

And let me give the other side of Dr. Berendzen's comments on foreign students. The fact that we have 50,000 foreign students enrolled in graduate science and engineering programs in our universities is a tribute to the perceived caliber worldwide of our educational institutions.

So we are still strong, and clearly we are doing some things right. But when you examine these figures in more depth, a clearer picture of our problems emerges. For example, we have to recognize our large national security responsibilities, and these require two-thirds of the federal R&D budget be devoted to defense.

So while 2.7 percent of GNP is devoted to R&D, the civilian R&D can claim only 1.9 percent, compared to 2.3 percent and 2.6 percent in Japan and West Germany, respectively. Now, no one knows just how significant these ratios are. But I think it is sobering to realize that Japan has set its sights on a 2.5

11

percent level by 1985 and a 3 percent level by 1990.

When it comes to the matter of industrial competitiveness, are even these figures the determinant of success? I don't think so. It seems to me that more important than the aggregate figures and the percentages is how effectively we use these R&D resources, how effectively we translate them into products and services that can truly determine our economic leadership.

Perhaps a different and more pointed analysis is warranted. If we look at the $100 billion, of this total 51 percent now comes from industry, 46 percent from the federal government. Another 2 percent comes from universities and 1 percent from nonprofit institutions. Less than 20 years ago the federal government had 65 percent and industry 33 percent. Now, I am not saying this change is bad, but it is a fact.

But also in those earlier days, the government R&D programs contributed more to the leading-edge research results applicable to competitiveness than they do today. Federal R&D, specifically the DOD's R&D, had more impact on advancing technologies of such industries as aerospace, computers, scientific instruments and even communications equipment. And these became and have remained among our strongest competitive industries.

Today, however, there are still major benefits to industry from the DOD R&D, but the R&D support by industry plays a much greater role in advancing the nation's technological prowess. And it is not only in the amount of R&D industry funds, but because that R&D is more of a leading-edge nature that contributes to our industrial competitiveness and at the same time to our military technology. That's true in such fields as electronics, communications, computers, biotechnology as well as medical and scientific instruments.

If you just look at the semiconductor business, the industry is driving that technology. And the federal government and the DOD are using that technology successfully for defense purposes. Again, I don't think this is bad. I think it is very, very good, and it is not a criticism of the federal government.

If our industry is strong, the defense sector can depend on those benefits. But this does say that we cannot consider the total $100 billion for R&D as being the effective size that we look at when we consider industrial competitiveness. Nor should we discount the total federal government contribution and say that only $51 billion is the number we should take. It is somewhere in between.

The main point of this is we cannot be complacent. Our R&D that is affecting our industrial competitiveness is not bigger

12

than the percent of GNP spent by the people we are competing with. And that says we must be concerned about its effectiveness -- how effective are the dollars we are spending.

In other words, we have to ask how can the government, with its $44 billion of R&D, best use those resources to influence industrial competitiveness. And what can industry, with its $49 billion, do better to translate the R&D into competitive products and services?

And perhaps more important, what can all of us-- government, industry, universities -- do together to make this essential process work best in the future, just as we have in the past?

Now, before trying to suggest some specific answers, let me acknowledge that much progress is indeed taking place in strengthening our underlying resources. If you attend meetings on R&D and industrial policy that are being held these days, if you read the material that is being written, you realize that, despite some differences, there is a growing consensus, there is a set of "conventional wisdoms" that has evolved.

Notable advisory groups, such as the President's Commission on Industrial Competitiveness, the White House Science Council, the Business-Higher Education Forum, have all agreed, among other things, on the nation's need to improve education at all levels, to increase support for university research, including the needs of graduate education, faculty and instrumentation.

We need to improve the interaction between universities and industry. We need to increase the incentives for industry investment both in R&D and in plant modernization. We need to reduce regulatory and antitrust inhibitions to further industrial R&D. We need to improve the protection of intellectual property. And we need to make more effective industrial use of the federal R&D dollars that are spent, especially those spent in the federal laboratories.

There is no doubt all these are important, and it is encouraging that we are pursuing action on many fronts. Let me mention some examples of these. The President's Commission on Industrial Competitiveness, on which I serve, to date has endorsed some 17 recommendations, all of which have been presented to the Cabinet Council on Commerce and Trade. And many are already in the form of legislation before or through Congress or are awaiting administrative action.

Now, these include legislation to modify the antitrust laws to encourage pro-competitive joint R&D ventures, to change the Freedom of Information Act to protect the rights of private firms regarding the release of commercially sensitive information, and to streamline patent laws and procedures.

The President's Commission has also recommended incentives to increase the number and quality of engineering graduate students and faculty members, and to increase funding for engineering equipment and research, including support for proposed research centers. And we have recommended measures to facilitate the use of computers in elementary and secondary education.

Now, these are only a few of the Commission's recommendations. They are, in fact, the immediate action items that we identified for the Administration to examine. The more fundamental recommendations will be coming out in the final report.

I mention the Business-Higher Education Forum. They have made a number of noteworthy recommendations in their Report to the President. Among these relevant to today's discussion, they recommend that we encourage R&D partnerships through clarification of the antitrust and tax policies; expand government funding for university-industry cooperation -- and particularly encourage universities and companies that have little past experience with this kind of cooperation.

They recommend that we identify new methods of transferring technology developed with government R&D funds to private industry. They also recommend that industry give more emphasis to manufacturing technology and upgrade the incentives for people to specialize in this technology.

They recommend that business schools expand their teaching and research on the elements of management that are fundamental to industrial R&D, to technological innovation, to productivity and to product quality. They also recommend that engineering schools reemphasize manufacturing engineering.

But above all of these, the Forum places the overall requirement that, and I quote, "As a nation we must develop a consensus that industrial competitiveness is crucial to our social and economic well-being." This is a very good statement!

Now, I believe we are achieving such a consensus, and we have already begun to act on many of the recommendations that I have mentioned. There is no shortage of good legislation on these matters. If you are close to Congress, you can see lots of it. And the federal agencies, such as the National Science Foundation, can point out numerous programs beginning to focus on these needs. I would include the Presidential Young Investigators Award, the initiative to create the engineering research centers, and programs that are stimulating partnerships among scientists and engineers in universities, federal laboratories and industry.

14

If you agree, then, that we are generally on the right track, let us get back to this $100 billion question. And let us get to the question of what can the government, the universities, and industries do to direct their R&D more effectively to achieve greater industrial competitiveness. Let me spend a few minutes on each sector, beginning as one likes to do, with the government.

When it comes to basic research, particularly that which builds the foundations for tomorrow's technologies, the universities remain our major source. At the same time, they supply the nation with its future researchers, faculty, and industrial scientists engineers. All this is still predominantly funded by the federal government.

Of the estimated $11.8 billion the country will spend in 1984 on basic research, about $7 billion will come from the federal government; about $2.5 billion will come from industry -- 10 percent of that, by the way, spent in my company. And the universities will spend about $1.2 billion of their own funds. That's the way it goes.

Now, where is this basic research support spent? The universities perform nearly one-half of all basic research, industry less than one-fifth; and the rest is largely in the federal laboratoies. It is crucial, then, that we direct these resources appropriately toward industrial needs.

Of course, you recognize, we all recognize, that a good portion of this federal money must go into such needs as health, national security and other endeavors that are clearly the government's responsibility. But I think we are also beginning to realize how much more our universities and federal labs could contribute to industry. It is essential that we focus more of this research and engineering talent on industrial innovation and productivity.

The Administration shows growing interest in engineering related to design and manufacturing. It is gratifying to hear the President's Science Advisor, Jay Keyworth, say, as he did at the AAAS R&D Colloquium last March: "We have been looking particularly at the broad areas of design and manufacturing because those are critical processes to master in converting knowledge into products."

And when he was examining the capabilties and needs of our universities in preparing students for today's environment in industry, he went on to say, "We are in the midst of a revolution in the way engineers work and the way modern industry operates. That resolution is putting potent computer tools and capabilities

15

in the hands of product designers, and the revolution is blurring the distinction between traditional disciplines."

This is the kind of thinking that has spearheaded the effort in the White House Science Office and elsewhere to create those university centers for cross-disciplinary education and research in engineering that I mentioned. This is a large and ambitious program. The National Academy of Engineering sees the possibility of eventually creating about 25 of these centers, which would involve at least 10 percent of the nation's engineering students. That's a big effort. Such centers will require continued strong disciplinary research programs at the universities. Therefore, the NSF has asked for a 22 percent increase in funds for engineering research.

Of course, it is also important that the instrumentation needs of university research are not being overlooked. And we have to recognize that the $400 million that the R&D agencies will contribute in 1985 is good, but it is not going to solve the total need.

Now, let me turn briefly to the matter of the federal laboratories, another potentially powerful contribution to our industrial competitiveness. The federal labs spend $18 billion, one-sixth of the nation's entire R&D funding and one-third of the federal R&D budget.

As you know, the missions and management of these laboratories have been under discussion for some time. The White House Science Council in 1982 convened a Federal Laboratory Review Panel, chaired by David Packard, to look into these matters.

One of its areas of recommendations deals with "Interactions with Universities, Industries and Users of Research Results." Specific recommendations the Panel made were that the "federal laboratories should encourage much more access to their facilities by universities and industry"; and that "R&D interactions between federal laboratories and industry should be greatly increased by more exchange of knowledge and personnel, collaborative projects, and industry funding of laboratory work, provided," they added, "an oversight mechanism is established to prevent unfair competitive practices."

I hope ways can be found to implement these recommendations quickly and effectively. But from all of these recommendations, you can see the government's effectiveness in supporting industrial competitiveness lies primarily in three areas -- the three obvious areas on sustaining a strong science and technology base, particularly in basic research; of optimizing the transfer of federally funded R&D results to industry; and, of course, of helping to ensure an adequate supply of technical people. Now, each of these roles relates closely to what happens in the universities, so let me turn to them next.

No nation in the world boasts a finer system of higher education. Our colleges and universities have a history of contribution to economic development in this country that is unmatched. Many of us tend to forget this point. I was fascinated to find it was eloquently expressed by Lord Bowden in his Graham Clark Lecture of 1967. Speaking about the role of the land grant colleges and universities, he said, "The idea that universities should study problems of applied science which were important to industry first took hold in the United States study all the significant problems of society ... We owe two-thirds of all the food which is grown today in the United States to new crops and new techniques which they developed and to the students whom they taught. They studied the Mechanics Arts, their ideas and their graduates transformed American industry, they transformed the very nature of a university, and they helped to create the world as we know it ... If I had to choose, I should say that this was the moment when our modern world began. For the first time in history, industry and agriculture were going to be studied in universities by scholars who believed that they should not ignore any of the problems of society."

A very powerful statement! Well, while I do not necessarily think we are again at such a momentous point in history as Lord Bowden described, I do think we are at a turning point or should be at a turning point in the relationships of universities to American industry. And in the past few years I think many significant things are happening in that relationship.

We are seeing a rising number of university-industry cooperative programs. We are seeing major industrial companies forming consortia to fund research at universities. We are seeing a growing number of industry-university joint ventures. And we are seeing a general increase in industry's contribution to research and education at universities.

Now, in some circles I know there is a concern that too much of this will divert or dilute the universities efforts in fundamental research. I do not think this need happen. There need be no "corruption" or "pure" research. In fact, to the contrary, I believe it is in the best interest of industry, as well as the universities, to keep the focus of university research as basic and as "leading edge" as possible. But the knowledge that discoveries in such research can contribute to society's economic and social gain should offer additional motivation to our university scientists.

Now let me pass the buck to industry with a few comments about my own sector's responsibilities. If the government and universities, indeed, should focus mainly on the support and transfer of basic research, and on the education and training of scientists and engineers, then where should industry concentrate?

While continuing its role of developing new technology and designing innovative products, industry's efforts should be on applying more of the intellect and power of today's R&D to industrial innovation, and particularly to the processes of production. There is a conventional wisdom that is emerging in response to the question, "What's happened to American industry?" It seems to me that the conventional wisdom is that it has lagged in its attention both to production and to the need to modernize manufacturing.

This situation is summed up exceptionally well by Professors Robert H. Hayes of Harvard and Steven C. Wheelright of Stanford in a recent book entitled Restoring Our Competitive Edge -- Competing Through Manufacturing.

They say: "There appears to have been a tacit agreement between firms in a number of important U.S. manufacturing industries over the past 15 - 20 years to compete primarily on dimensions other than manufacturing ability. The United States thought it had, as John Kenneth Galbraith (1958) phrased it, 'solved the problem of production.' Therefore, attention and resources have been directed toward mass distribution, packaging, advertising, and the development of incremental new products to round out existing product lines or to attack specific market segments, instead of toward improving manufacturing capabilities. The best managerial talent has been directed toward 'fast tracks' that often ignored or excluded direct manufacturing experience."

It is a very powerful book that they have written, and I recommend to you specifically the first chapter.

Now, if this is indeed the case, where does salvation lie? In some companies I think it lies in changes in management attitudes -- particularly in the need to recognize long-term requirements, including those of R&D, and to upgrade the technological capability of top management. This even includes the need to hire more people with engineering-scientific backgrounds as candidates for these top positions.

But, secondly, salvation lies in many industries in applying more R&D and systems engineering techniques to the total innovation process. Now, let me talk just a little bit about that. Four prime functions contribute to the total innovative process. They are research, development, production, and marketing and sales. High technology enterprises must be at the leading edge in all four of these to maintain a worldwide

18

competitive position.

Ideally, to achieve maximum competitiveness, two things must happen in these companies. First, each of these discrete functions must be given the individual attention and support it needs to be at the leading edge. But, second, all four must be organized into a total process, with information flowing among them, so they are mutually supportive and contribute to the successful design and manufacture of a competitive product.

I want to take a few minutes to talk about this process, for this is one that many U.S. industries are focusing on today with a great sense of urgency. At AT&T, we call this total process, for lack of anything more imaginative, the "Product Realization Process." I hope you will see, when I talk about this, that the fancy name does mean more than just product development.

We look at product realization as a total systems approach to producing products and services. It not only employs R&D in the creation of new products, but brings the discipline of R&D into the factory. It blends operations research, systems engineering, design automation and factory automation in an integrated systems approach to manufacturing. This, I will submit to you, is a very new challenge for those of us who manage R&D.

In this product realization approach, design and manufacturing must work in parallel, with information flowing back and forth continuously. This provides many advantages. Products are designed to be more easily manufactured, and the designs tend to be more nearly error free.

The process recognizes that the cost in manufacturing is heavily determined by relationships between information flow and material flow. As you know, high inventory cost is frequently more of a problem today than high labor cost. If you can get the information flow under control, the material flow will follow. In this sense, information serves in the factory today as a strategic resource.

In the product realization process, design automation and factory automation are critical. And in this area, as well as others, software is playing an increasingly important role in the factory. You have to couple design systems directly to companion manufacturing systems. It is nonsense to have CAD that dumps out paper, which in turn is fed into CAM in order to go to the next step. Instead, we must integrate computer aids to design, engineering, testing and manufacturing. And this integration has to be a dynamic process because the technologies, both of design and of production, are constantly and somewhat independently evolving.

19

Now, in some industries, such as the semiconductor industry, the integration of product design and process design has been a way of life -- for two decades. You cannot just design a 256K memory and have it manufactured. The process is essential to whether you can make it at all. But in other areas of industry this integrated process is a totally new concept. In what we used to call our assembly wire and test factories in Western Electric, this is an entirely new concept.

For all industries the progress in information technology is a major opportunity. Of course, for those of us in R&D, it is a new challenge and a new responsibility. And I think we have an important contribution to make in bringing the disciplines of R&D right into the production process.

In summary, these are some of the things that I think industry should do and is, in fact, beginning to do. But we will also continue to look to government to provide the proper economic climate and incentives to permit us to this work. We will continue to look to the universities to conduct much of the basic research underlying our newest technologies and to train the needed scientists and engineers.

And that brings me back to the theme of your conference. We have to work together in a total effort. I think we are moving in the right direction. But this global contest in industrial competitiveness has just begun, and our leadership in it is critical to America's long-term success -- economically, socially and politically. We cannot, and must not, be complacent. We must continue to improve and to develop all of our resources.

I appreciate the opportunity of sharing these thoughts with you today, and I hope they will be helpful in stimulating further discussion during what I believe is a very important conference to us and to the nation.

DISCUSSION

DR. HOGAN: Thank you very much, Dr. Ross. That was a very excellent summary of where we stand today and how things seem to be moving. Could you take time for a few questions now?

DR. WAKS: Dr. Ross, my name is Norman Waks, Mitre Corporation, a nonprofit systems engineering corporation. You made the point that two-thirds of the government's substantial budget, 44, 45 billion dollars out of your 100, is devoted to national security, which a number of people tend to feel is either all or a significant portion of loss in this industrial competitiveness area.

Last year a member of my panel, the DOD Head of Research and Advanced Technology, Dr. Edith Martin, stressed that a major, if not the primary, goal of defense R&D was to further the technology transfer process, particularly as regards manufacturing technology and manufacturing processes.

My question to you, as a follow-up to her statement of that goal, is whether or not you see this taking place out of the national security R&D effort to any great extent?

DR. ROSS: Well, I guest I have to disagree with her. I see the primary purpose of the security R&D being to further defense of the nation, and that is what it should be. And I certainly see attention being paid secondary to that.

DR. WAKS: That's very important, but not primary.

DR. ROSS: But the prime mission is to get the defense in order, and that is great. Now, what I see from where I sit, is that the DOD is using more of industry's technology than industry is using DOD technology, and I have no complaint with that.

All I am saying is, let us not fool ourselves that the whole $100 billion is that which is competitive with Japan. And I am not saying we should cut back on our defense R&D. Nor am I saying we should resector or there is anything wrong with the quality of it.

DR. WAKS: But you are not seeing the technological transfer fallout that she stressed was a goal?

DR. ROSS: I think within most of the technologies we are delaing with, the universities and industries are leading DOD, not the other way around.

DR. WALKER: Dr. Ross, my name is Walker. I am from Penn State. You have started out by saying that the country is spending a great deal of money on R&D and that the universities, industry and government ought to make sure that the country is getting its money's worth.

I am going to express an opinion that the universities are not doing a very good job at this. The universities are supposed to take this money and through their graduate schools and their research efforts -- and the two cannot be separated -- make sure the country gets its money's worth.

Now, years ago we used to say that universities produced new knowledge and people who have knowledge. And 30 years ago most of our graduate students were products of our own universities, who came into the university, got master's degrees, doctor's degrees, and went into industry or into teaching.

Today, more than half of our graduate students are not native born. They are trained in foreign universities. Some of them intend to enter American industry, and they usually do it after a fairly long delay, naturalization, security, language difficulties -- but probably a third of them go into American industry.

Some of them go back to their own countries and we can regard that as a contribution to developing nations, if the nations can use them. But too many of them stay on and get doctor's degrees, go back to their own countries, and cannot fit into their countries' economies.

For instance, a young man who spends seven years getting a doctor's degree on robotic control goes back to Ghana, and they have never seen or heard of a robot. And he becomes a taxi driver and tour guide, and that seven years is lost not just for the country, but for the whole world.

Well, you say, why are there so many people who are in this classification as research associates and teaching assistants in the universities?

The number of American-born people staying on for doctor's degrees in engineering is going down and down. And part of the reason is that they are ill paid as research assistants, but also a good many of them say there isn't much point in staying on to get a master's degree or a doctor's degree. "I can go into industry, spend the same amount of time, and learn just as much. And I may not have that union card, but it doesn't mean very much anyway."

We have to find a way to have more of our people stay on and get doctor's degrees, do advanced R&D, get to the frontiers of knowledge and then go into industry. My question is, how can we do it?

DR. ROSS: I think your observations are quite correct. You know, one of my great friends -- who just retired from being the President of the Communications Workers of America -- said, "To every complicated problem there is a simple answer, and it is wrong." And I think you have one of these.

It is very distressing to see what you see, and there are things that need to be done. Now, in my view, we in industry have contributed to this.

In the '60's, we got into such intense competition for engineers we started creaming them off at the bachelor's level with the offer that "We will take the top of the class now, and we will put you through graduate school free." And we are doing it; everybody else is. We trapped ourselves into it.

When I first came into the business, you came to the company with all of the diplomas you were going to get. Now you come into companies with an entitlement to further education. There is no question that we are taking some of the brighter people, the brightest people, out of the universities at the bachelor's level. I do not know how to work our way out of that, but I wish we could.

As I see it, one of the consequences is that the U.S. citizens who stay on in graduate school are those who really want to go on to Ph.D's or the ones who cannot get job offers at the bachelor's level. And that latter situation is not good.

So we find ourselves, for example, hiring heavily at the bachelor's level and heavily at the Ph.D. level. I am a little puzzled about the master's degree types as to nationality, because a lot of them are not immediately hireable --you are quite correct. You have to do some rather strange things to get them these visas,so that is a problem. I would also like to see us change our educational inducements.

Now, one thing we did in my company -- and I am proud of it -- when sending our employees back to college full-time for a year to get a master's degree, was to match tuition. We have stopped doing that and have put the funds into supporting 100 Ph.D. students in the universities.

Our intention is that they will not come and work for Bell Labs. Our hope is they will stay in the universities. If they do not want to stay in the universities, we would rather they come work for us than IBM, but that is another matter. But I think that is the kind of thing we can do.

Let me make an uneducated observation. It takes an awfully long time to go from being a freshman in engineering or physics to getting a Ph.D. Need it take that long? Isn't that a terrific investment that you are asking people to put in at a very creative, very early stage in their lives? I think one ought to re-examine the question of whether you have to take that long. There is just so much information people need to be useful. I am making a speech in response to your speech. I do not know the answer.

Something also has to be done about salaries. It has been done in the business schools. It has been done in the law schools. Why cannot similar things be done to raise the salaries in the science and technology departments of the schools? I do not know the answer. I am not an expert in universities. I agree with you problem.

DR. BARNES: Dennis Barnes, University of Virginia. Our keynote speaker last year was Roland Schmitt of General Electric. He commented on manufacturing technology legislation which was then going through the Congress and pointed out he thought it was probably a bad idea because, primarily, it would distort what industry would do on its own and that he had little belief that the government was probably able to chose where the emphasis ought to be put.

That was very disconcerting to me at the time because I had just returned from the Senate Commerce Committee, where the legislation originated and had had a hand in writing it, I would have to admit, in reluctant collaboration with the White House, which shared a lot of those reservations at the time also. The question is, do you share any of Dr. Schmitt's reservations?

DR. ROSS: Well, I read his talk and thought it was a very, very fine talk. It scared me when I read it. And I agree with what he was saying. What he was saying is that he does not believe the people in Washington should decide which technologies are important and which should be developed. I agree with that entirely.

And I think what you see developing around here, around the nation, is the belief that we should stimulate total innovation, total R&D -- whether increased R&D in industry, increased investment in the manufacturing process -- but not have somebody say which way it should be done. We should leave it to the private enterprise system to pick and choose what should be done.

I think we are also saying that as far as the universities are concerned, for goodness' sake, let us increase the total funding to them, but let us not make it directed funding. I can agree with that. I do not see any conflict with that.

DR. BAEDER: Don Baeder from Occidental Petroleum. I would like to continue on this latter issue. Look, I have a feeling that we have a really great R&D system within the country that is truly poised to move. And why we haven't moved hasn't been because of the R&D competitiveness; it has been because of the industry competitiveness in those sectors.

I would strongly urge the Commission on Industrial Research and Development to go much beneath the surface, to look back and again to examine why certain of our industries really have gotten into this noncompetitive nature.

Let me give you an example of where I think we have an extremely competitive system. It is like exploration and production for oil. There is not a country in the world that can match us, not a one. We are finding it in smaller pockets. We are going to places drilling wells in thousand so feet of water. It is an unbelievable system.

You get into the undersea technology that has been developed, the closures on the bottom of the ocean. Well, great. Why? Because when the government puts up some tracts for bidding, there are 50 bidders out there from all over the world. It's a competitive game. And where there's a competitive game, the management of industry goes back and uses what it needs to do to win, and it goes back and it supports technology. It gets great university programs in sensing brought into this.

Now, let us take the steel industry. What did the steel industry do during the last twenty years? It decimated a beautiful research organization it used to have. It had a fine basic research crew.

What did the industry do? It went along and buckled to the demands of labor. There were industry contracts. Every one of the competitors raised prices in tandem with each other. All of a sudden they got wages up to twenty-five bucks. The processes are old. They have not revamped them. There was no need to.

All of a sudden the dollar started to shrink. That's the only way they maintained their competitiveness. The dollar started to strengthen, and we are plagued with imports from countries. We complain about the dollar. The dollar ought to be strong. Be proud of where that dollar is today.

What we ought to be worrying about is what are we going to do to really get the industry competitive. I think if we do have that R&D machine tuned they are going to use it, and I would like your comments on this.

DR. ROSS: We have wrestled with just this on the Commission's Committee on Research, Development and Manufacturing. We think that the R&D, in terms of quality, is in good shape. We think, in terms of quantity, it can be competitive, but we should not be complacent.

I think the only concern we have there, and we are wrestling with that concern at the moment, is we do not quite see the focus for R&D, the forum for R&D, in the nation that would assure us that indeed we are putting all of the right thinking into how it should be managed, and particularly the federal government's R&D. So we are looking for some forum that would make this so-called scientific community a reality in Washington. But apart from that, I agree with you.

Now, the issue of industrial competitiveness -- no question, the ability to translate technology into competitive product is where we have selectively done poorly, but only selectively.

And you mentioned one industry that is doing very well. Let me mention the semiconductor industry, whether it be in the Silicon Valley or the Lehigh Valley. That is an industry that is R&D-intensive, capital-intensive. We have put the money in there and are doing very well. The Japanese are good implementers, but they are not ahead of us.

Now, you take two industries -- you mentioned steel; I mentioned semiconductors. Why is one so progressive and the other not doing so well? They are working with the same inflation rate, the same rate of exchange, the same cost of money. They are working with the same capital structures, the same tax laws, the same antitrust laws. Why does one succeed and the other does not? That has been a real puzzlement to the people on my committee.

One of the things that we are beginning to feel -- and it is a strange, nebulous thing -- is that it gets back to the attitudes of management, the attitudes in the board room, and the attitudes of the security analysts. And how do we turn all of those around?

You know, I managed a pension fund for a company. We set up three pension fund managers, put them in competition, and looked at them each year. If one of them was not doing well, we threw him out.

Now, those managers are going to be investing in things that have increased earnings quarter by quarter by quarter. And that puts pressure in the board room not to put your investment in things that pay off ten years from now. Somehow, we have to turn that around. And I do think there has to be an understanding in industry that it is in industry's interest, in the nation's interest, to take a longer-term view, not a shorter-term view. People must think more broadly about their responsibilites in the board rooms.

Now, we think there may be some tax incentives or some tax leveling. There may be, but I really think the basic thing is going to come down to some attitudes, attitudes coming out of the universities, out of the Harvard Business School. Is that really the "now" generation that is in the board room? I am very, very puzzled by the fact that within the same environment one company succeeds and the other does not. I would be very interested in anybody else's comments on this because we need help.

DR. PFEIFFER: Heinz Pfeiffer, Pennsylvania Power and Light Company. I have a question that really goes back to the attitude with quite a different slant on it. About 40 years ago I went to work for one of the major laboratories, and people at that time were hired because of the assessment of them as individuals. And continuing their thesis was a no-no.

And more and more I see the big laboratories, perhaps even your own, hiring people because of specific skills that come out of their Ph.D.'s rather than hiring them more broadly based on your view of their potential. I would like your comments on that.

DR. ROSS: Well, I can only speak from the point of view of a big company. And we have and continue to hire the well-educated, whole person because we know very well that whatever that specialty is, it is good for five years -- at the most ten -- and then that person has to do something very, very different. So we have not shifted.

Now, many small companies that hire a dozen engineers hire programmers and operations research people, and expect them to come on the job and contribute on that job immediately. I do not know what you do about that. But I think, in the bigger companies which still contribute to the basic technology, we are doing it the right way.

DR. PFEIFFER: I think I have seen a real shift.

DR. ROSS: Have you really?

DR. PFEIFFER: Yes.

DR. ROSS: I hope you have not seen it in my company.

27

DR. PFEIFFER: Well, I do not know your company. I almost went to work for them.

DR. ROSS: By the way, a comment was made somewhere about the quality of the engineers and scientists coming into business. In my company, we are delighted with what is coming into our business, really -- dedicated people, well trained, hard working. I can suggest ways to improve the quality of the, but that is not our complaint.

The worry is, are we eating out own seed corn, and will this quality continue? But at the moment we are very satisfied with the output of the universities, not the high schools, but then we do not hire high school graduates.

DR. PFEIFFER: But industry hires the teachers.

DR. ROSS: Not too much. We do not. We compete for them -- you are quite right -- but are the high schools paying competitive salaries?

DR. PFEIFFER: No, but I am saying it is part of the reason for the possibility of some difficulties.

DR. ROSS: Yes, but in the end do you not think everybody should pay competitive salaries?

DR. PFEIFFER: I think we should find some way to improve the situation. We are all responsible.

DR. ROSS: I agree with you, and I am on the PTA, too.

DR. COOK: Charles Cook from Bechtel. The problem in the manufacturing sector, at least to a certain industry, has recently been addressed by several. It is sort of a puzzlement why it is with supposedly uniform rules, regulation, tax structures, so on, that certain industries can remain competitive. It is not so hard to see why the electronics industry would when it is growing so rapidly.

It is more appropriate to focus on those industries that are not in a rapid growth mode. When we look at many of them, as has been done by the Manufacturing Research Center at the University of Florida, an interesting facet of our tax laws becomes apparent.

Evidently, if their figures are correct -- and I cannot quote them exactly -- it costs a manufacturer of consumer goods roughly three times as much as the expense of providing research for the development of new products than one would expect because of the rules and regulations and the tax laws.

This is not so in the aircraft industry, where certain benefits accrue. Government subsidies, in effect, change the ratio rather strikingly. And it is very clear from the figures collected that there is a fairly strong correlation between the success of an industry and the ratio of the expense and the real expense -- not the cost of the research activity, but the real expense to the company in terms of cost of research, the tax calculations, requirements associated with it, and so on, and the international competitive status of that industry. These figures are so spectacular they are hard to ignore.

Price Waterhouse and others are looking at some of the so-called standard accounting procedures. In this regard, they find that there are reasons apparently why certain industries have not been competitive, and these are all monetary. Would you care to comment on what the President's Commission is doing with regard to this aspect of the problem?

DR. ROSS: Well, firstly, you are saying there are some studies that demonstrate that our tax laws are disfavoring R&D in certain industries?

DR. COOK: Yes, it makes it very difficult in certain areas where we compete internationally.

DR. ROSS: If you have such a document, I wish you would send it to me because we have been looking for such material. The Commission does have a Financial Subcommittee, which I am not a member of, which has some very fine experts. They are looking into just this area, and we have stressed to them that we have to understand the tax incentives and disincentives, both to R&D and to production modernization. I do not know what stage they are up to, but I have not heard that they have any "golden relays," as we call them in our industry.

Egils, could you comment on that? You are closer to it. This is Egils Milbergs, Deputy Director of the Commission.

DR. MILBERGS: Well, Ian, you are quite correct. One of the committees, the Capital Resources Committee of the Commission, essentially has been evaluating the functioning of our tax system as we look at industry by industry.

We are coming out with two conclusions: one, that in the United States, relative to our competitors -- let us take Japan as an example -- we have seen our cost of capital to be about two or three times the cost in Japan.

There are a number of explanations for that, not just nominal interest rates, but the tax system in Japan, debt-equity ratios and so on. But, nevertheless, our industries have been at a competitive disadvantage in the '70's, particularly our manufacturing industry, becuase of the wide differential in the cost of capital.

The second issue they have been evaluating along these lines, Ian, is how our tax system has differential impacts, depending on what industry you look at -- in other words, the non-neutrality of our tax system.

For example, some industries would end up paying an effective 80 or 90 percent marginal tax rate, depending upon certain kinds of investments made. Maybe Charlie's comment was referring to a kind of industry in which -- given its capital structure, expenses, and so on -- that tax rate is quite expensive, along with maybe certain regulatory hurdles that will have to be crossed as well.

But, indeed, our taxes for our industry create anywhere from 20 to 30 percent direct subsidy. So we have this tremendous variation in terms of how our tax system affects cost of capital, as well as provides a different kind of marginal tax rate for different industries.

Consequently, what this committee is trying to come up with is some proposal with respect to our tax system. I would suspect they would be trying to move the tax system toward more neutrality, and this begins to start putting you into looking very seriously at the various kinds of flat tax, as well as value-added tax type proposals. I can only predict what will happen October 23rd at our Dallas meeting, but the subject will certainly be presented.

DR. MORAN: I am David Moran. I come from the Naval Ship Research and Development Laboratory, which is a federal defense R&D laboratory. You mentioned the difference between the industrial contribution to federal programs as opposed to the federal laboratory contribution to industrial research.

In addition to the regulations which control federal R&D laboratories, I think there may be some differences in incentives -- and perhaps even lack of incentive -- within the federal laboratories for support of industrial research. I would like to ask if you can see some of those incentives and perhaps some of the ones that can be changes in the federal laboratories?

DR. ROSS: What kinds of incentives are you talking about?

DR. MORAN: Some of them are perhaps personal. We have nothing in the federal laboratories that is equivalent to the profit motive.

DR. ROSS: I think we have not talked about incentives to pedal the technology outside of the main mission, and I would worry about that. I think laboratories, whether they are industry or government laboratories, ought to have a clear mission. Everybody in them should be dedicated to that mission, and I worry about people getting diverted from that mission.

Now, there are some people you wouldn't like who say that the federal laboratories' budget should be cut. And one way to counteract that is for the federal laboratories to not only accomplish their own missions, but demonstrate to industry that they have good technology which is useful to industry. That is one incentive.

But let me turn the thing the other way around. If we are going to get good interaction between industry and the federal laboratories, where we do not now have it, I think you have to have good R&D in those industries.

There are lots of good reactions going on, and they are probably in the industries that are not having problems with transfer of technology.

We are picking on the steel industry, but the steel industry does not have a great interaction with federal laboratories and really does not have the receivers to do it.

In my view, the best way you get this good interaction is for the bright people in industry R&D to get to know the bright people in federal R&D -- so that they deal with each other the way you do in any R&D community and see what is in it for both sides. I have seen that work time and time again. And I think the final incentive there is the professional desire to get the job done in the most effective way. That is the way I would hope it would go.

Now, I do despair of somebody coming and and saying, "Such and such a laboratory, you have to go work with the steel industry or the garment industry." There is nothing to work into. But we have no proposals other than somehow working this into the charter of the director of your lab, unless you are the director of your lab, to put some emphasis in that.

Now, maybe this is an area where some better focus in Washington on the total federal R&D spending might be helpful. Suppose there were some place that worried about industrial competitiveness and asked your lab, "Okay, you are doing a fine job building ships or whatever you do, but what do you have in there that also would be an offshoot to the automobile industry or something else?" Maybe we need some of that, too.

31

DR. SORROWS: My name is Howard Sorrows. I am from the National Bureau of Standards, also a government laboratory.

DR. ROSS: A very fine one.

DR. SORROWS: Thank you. I read several months ago an article about AT&T in which they said that the managers in general came from a liberal arts background rather than from a technical background, which surprised, I guess, a lot of people. And I am sure that is not true in the Bell Laboratories, but I would like your comments on whether or not you think that in general maybe some of the universities do not have quite the right curriculum for what you might call the real productive areas of our industry?

DR. ROSS: What are the real productive areas of our industry?

DR. SORROWS: I'm talking about where they actually make and sell the products.

DR. ROSS: Well, a lot of my bosses came out with liberal arts educations. Remember, in a business that -- before we were "helped" by the government -- had a million employees, 800,000 of those were operating telephone company people. And many of them started their careers climbing telephone poles.

Regarding liberal arts, I do not think we make enough use of the output of liberal arts colleges. Well-educated people who can read and write are a great asset, and many of the engineers who come into my business do not read and write very well.

One of the companies of which I am a board member has a program to go out and hire liberal arts graduates because they think they can hire better people than they can from the engineering schools, not because they are brighter people, but because they can compete better.

But you are talking about scientists and engineers. That raises a distressing point. If you look at the IEEE survey that came out recently on the members of IEEE and how they felt about their profession, they ranked the kind of work they liked to do -- and at the bottom was manufacturing-engineering.

Now, where does all that start? Some of it starts in the universities. Some of it is bred in industry, where maybe you pay your manufacturing engineer less than you pay your research scientist. But there also has always been a tendency in the university -- forgive me -- to say that the most noble thing you can do when you graduate is to stay in the university and do research and teach. If you cannot do that, go into industry, but

32

do research. And maybe you will come back to us. The last thing you should do is go into a factory.

Now, I think somehow or another we should turn that around, and maybe it means we need to get a better relationship between the manufacturing parts of our industries and the schools from which they are taking people.

Now, that does not mean to me we should move toward vocational training in the universities. I think that would be very, very bad. I think we need people who are educated in the basic sciences, as much as you can get in the years that we can afford. But somehow or other they ought to feel it is noble to go into manufacturing. Maybe what we need is co-op programs, sabbaticals, that will bring bright professors into factories and factory people into universities.

CHAPTER THREE
"Quantitative S&T Overview"

Dr. C. E. Falk
National Science Foundation

To start out, let me disappoint you a little. I am not going to talk about U.S. science and technology but about U.S. research and development because the main theme of this conference is the assessment of the impact of federal R&D funding on the overall United States performance in these important activities. Clearly this is an extremely comprehensive topic and one which will draw a lot of discussion. It has many facets, some of them micro, some of them macro, with many already brought out this morning in Dr. Ross' address.

It is clear that conference participants are going to have different perceptions of what is happening in the R&D picture and that is good because it will stimulate a lively discussion. However, sometimes there is unnecessary discussion of opinions when facts are available. Consequently, my objective this morning is to try to establish a factual basis for our sessions. Hopefully, this will prevent debates which facts can resolve.

One aspect which lends itself particularly well to such a factual approach is the question of how much R&D is being funded in the United States and what changes occurred during the last ten years. Furthermore, if one translates the funding to constant dollars, that is take out the effect of inflation, then one can even take the next step and interpret these funding levels as reflections of the levels of R&D activity. This is, of course, the most important aspect, not the money itself, but what is being done with it. Consequently, I will steer you through a set of R&D constant dollar funding charts which will give you an idea of what has been happening over the last ten years.

I will not only be talking about what has been happening in terms of federal funding of R&D, which is usually expressed in "obligations," but will cover all sources and performers. Consequently, my frame of reference will be "expenditures" because the data we collect from the non-federal components of the economy come to us in these terms, i.e., how much money these sectors actually spent. The one slight disadvantage of this approach is that one cannot go quite as far in time as one could with obligations. For example, right now we have a pretty good idea of the federal R&D obligations for fiscal '85. However, as you will notice from my charts, the most current figures will usually be for 1984 expenditures and those expenditures really reflect what happened in terms of federal obligations a year or two earlier. This is an important factor to keep in mind.

Since you are interested in what happened in the most recent periods, my analyses will generally compare the 1975 to 1980 period with that of 1980 to 1984.

Chart 1 provides an overview of the national R&D effort. The federal sector is depicted in black, while the private sector, mostly industry, is cross-hatched. This type of coding will be used in all charts. If one looks at the left bar one will note that the government provides a little less than half of all the R&D money in the United States but that the principal source is industry, which supplies 51 percent of R&D funds.

On the other hand, if one looks at the middle bar, one will observe that when it comes to the performance of R&D, federal laboratories carry out only eleven percent and industry is the primary R&D performer responsible for the three-quarters of all American research and development.

It is also important to be aware of the relative magnitude of various R&D components. The bar on the right shows that almost two-thirds of U.S. R&D funding goes into development, while research makes up the other third, with about one-tenth going to basic research and about twenty percent of the total going into applied research.

Another feature to be kept in mind before examining detailed changes on national totals is shown in Chart 2, namely the distribution of the federal government's R&D funding in terms of its perceived functional objectives. This chart is shown with three time frames. The top bar represents the 1974 picture, the next lower one 1979, and finally the lowest one 1984. Keep in mind that the bottom box is in millions of dollars and the top box is in billions -- and that everything is depicted in 1972 constant dollars.

What one immediately notices is not only that defense R&D constitutes the major component of federal R&D funding, but that it is the only one that has increased since 1979 and that this increase is quite large, about 50 percent. As for the other functions shown, most have maintained relatively constant levels since 1979 with two exceptions. Energy R&D funding has decreased significantly during this period. This is primarily the result of the current federal policy that expects government involvement to be minimal in R&D areas which are most suitable for the prviate sector in view of the latter's direct output and knowledge of the market place. This policy has resulted in reductions in energy development efforts, especially in the area of demonstration projects. The other functional funding level that has gone down somewhat deals with natural resources and environment.

Now, let us examine the effects of these functional funding changes on various facets of national R&D funding (Chart 3). Since your focus will be on recent times, I have developed sets of compound charts. Let me take a little time to walk you through the first one because there will be lots of others.

Sources of R&D Funding

Generally, on the left is a conventional type of line chart, in this case national R&D expenditures by source. This type of chart is most useful to detect major trend changes and also to place the relative magnitude of various components into perspective. What one sees in this chart, for example, is that 1977 was a key year in the relationship between federal and private R&D funding because the two lines crossed and from then on non-federal funding has exceeded the federal contribution. Previously the government had funded much more of the national R&D effort, as much as two-thirds in 1968. After the cross-over occurred the gap has increased steadily. By 1985 the proportion of the national R&D effort supported by the government is expected to be 46 percent, while industry, the largest sectoral funding source, will provide 51 percent.

What a line chart cannot show well are small changes: it is very hard to see a change in slope. The chart on the right, however, accomplishes this by showing annual rates of change in the funding.

The way to look at this chart is to focus on shading and observe the kind of a pattern that develops. Such a procedure shows, for example, that the rates of increase in the federal funding of R&D have generally been smaller than those of the private sector. One will also notice that the black bars, which represent the governmental changes, constantly increased during the second half of the decade to 5.1 percent in 1984. That increase is very heavily driven by what was shown in the previous chart (Chart 2), namely major increases in defense R&D. Defense R&D constitutes two-thirds of the increase in 1984 federal R&D funding and this pattern is repeated in fiscal year 1985.

Annual growth in Federal R&D defense funding has actually averaged about 11 percent in constant dollars over this 1980-84 period, while the overall governmental annual R&D expenditure rate has been about four to five percent. That means that something else had to go down. What decreased was the civilian R&D component, which actually went down by about five percent per year during this period.

Now, looking at the overall nonfederal component of the R&D

funding picture one can see immediately that the rates of increase during the whole ten-year period have been larger for the private sector than they were for government. Also, one can observe somewhat of a compensatory pattern. If one looks at the second half, from 1980 to 1984, when the governmental part had been increasing, one will note that the private sector has been increasing too, but not quite as much as it did before. One will see this pattern in most of these charts; there generally seems to be some compensation. One possible explanation could be that the system can just take so much of an increase and that therefore, when one component increases significantly over an extended period the other one will only increase at a slower rate.

You will also notice in this and most of the other charts a little dip in non-federal growth rates in 1983. That is a reflection of the 1982 recession which did cause industry to pause a little in its R&D spending, but only for one year and now that spending is increasing again very significantly.

Having discussed this pattern of the major sectoral sources of R&D money, let us look at the national totals. Not surprisingly, since everything else has been going up, the total has been growing, too. The increases during the second half of the decade are a little higher, but overall, during the whole decade, total R&D in the United States in constant dollars has been going up at about four and a half percent per year.

Type of R&D Activities

Having looked at the pattern of funding sources for the overall R&D effort, let us now examine what has happened to the different types of R&D activity. The line chart portion of this chart for development (Chart 4) shows that in development the gap between the government and the private sector increased between 1975 and 1980. However, since then the two have been going up at about the same robust rate. The government part in recent years has been concentrated on funding defense related development in industrial companies and government laboratories.

With respect to industrial funding of development one can see the same pattern mentioned before. Industrial development funding increased at almost twice the governmental rate between 1970 and 1980 but since then, as the government increased its rate of development funding, the industrial rates pulled back a little. As for total national development activity, it has gone up somewhat more rapidly during the recent years than it did during the later part of the seventies, primarily because of the acceleration of government funding.

Looking at applied research (Chart 5), one sees a somewhat

37

different picture. The line chart shows that the federal government's funding of applied research has stayed almost level, especially during the last four or five years, while the non-federal component has continued to increase at a very healthy rate. This federal funding pattern reflects the Administration's policy which I mentioned previously when discussing development, namely of leaving to the private sector the applied research which is related to its type of products and processes. The government thus is focusing its applied research funds on areas which are primarily Federal responsibilities. The bar chart shows that during the last four to five year period applied research funding by the government has stayed about constant but that industrial funding of this activity has moved up very smartly. Apparently the government policy seems to be working, the private sector is picking up the bill for its increased applied research needs.

Looking at basic research (Chart 6), we have again a different situation. The line chart shows that instead of contributing less than half of the total, as is the case in development and applied research, the federal government provides two-thirds of basic research funding. Futhermore, if one reviews the annual rates of change, both the federal and private funding show increasing rates of growth, though it should be notes that governmental funding of basic research during the 1975 to 1980 period was increasing somewhat more rapidly than it did during the last five years. During this latter period there was actually a little decrease in the early years but since then federal basic research funding has been growing at an increasing rate with the 1984 increase being of the order of seven percent. Furthermore, the 1984/85 increase will again be of that magnitude. Thus, the pattern of federal basic research funding increases is U-shaped. The rate of increase was fairly high in 1978, then started to go down, hit bottom in the early 80's, but since then has been going up. In this case, since the government is such a major contributor, one does not see quite the compensating effect evident in the previous charts. Nevertheless, there seems to be some compensation. One certainly can notice that between 1980 and 1984 the non-federal rates of increase are still fairly high, on the order of four to five percent per year, and they continue to go up. Incidentally, these increases evolve about equally from the universities and colleges themselves (which frequently means from the states) and the industrial sector.

Sectoral Performance

Having looked at the components of R&D, let us examine how the various sectors that perform R&D are affected by the funding patterns of the various sources. But first, since the focus of this conference is on the Federal Government, Chart 7 shows to what sectors the federal R&D funds have been channeled. What one notices is that Federal funding of industrial R&D increased at an accelerated rate during the 80-85 period. This is really not surprising if one recalls that a significant fraction of the increase in federal R&D funding was being directed towards defense. Furthermore, an increasing proportion of defense R&D funding is in development. And where is development predominantly carried out? In the industrial sector. So it is not surprising that the Federal increases of industrial R&D are somewhat higher in the second half of the last decade than they were in the first.

With respect to federal support of academic research, the first half was a little better than the second half. The average rate of change was plus 2.8 percent between 1975 and 1980, but only of the 1.3 percent per year since the, including some negative dips in the early 80's. It is worthwhile noting that only in 1984 did the rate of increase really shoot up significantly. This occurs, of course, because most of the federally funded basic research is carried out in academia and Federal basic research funding increased significantly in 1984 (Chart 6). This trend will continue into 1985.

Now let us examine what happens to the sectors in toto, that is, when one considers all funding sources, not only the government. In industry (Chart 8) one can see a pretty healthy pattern. The overall rate of increase went up until 1980. Since then it has gone down a little, but on average the increases in the second half of this decade are certainly larger. A major reason again is governmental funding. However, industry itself has also responded quite strongly to the general challenges of R&D and has been increasing its own funds considerably.

With respect to academia (Chart 9), which is very little involved in development but mostly in research, one can notice that the funding pattern pretty much followed the federal pattern of research funding. This is the case because, as shown by the line chart, two-thirds of academic research funds originate in the federal government. However, less than one may think goes into basic research. There is a common conception that academia is only engaged in basic research and that is just not so. Actually one-third of all academic research expenditures are spent in the area of applied research. I suspect that the proportion is going to be increasing in view of the increases in university-industry cooperative efforts which are taking place now.

The pattern of overall academic research expenditures follows pretty much the pattern of changes in governmental research funds made available to universities and again one will note that rates of change follow a U-type curve during the last five years. The last few years show a trend of fairly large increases. The 1984 increase is of the order of almost nine percent in constant dollars and that increase is going to be fairly similar.

Summary

I have presented a lot of data at a very high information density. I do not want to conclude this presentation without giving a broad overview of what has been happening. Consequently, Chart 10 provides such an impressionistic overview. The double arrows represent annual increases greater than four percent in constant dollars; the single arrows stand for increases between one and four percent; the horizontal arrows show changes in the plus to minus one percent range.

The first impression when one looks at this chart -- especially if one looks at the last column on the right, which depicts what happened to the total R&D picture -- is that there are a lot of double arrows. This means that the overall national R&D effort as well as its various components have done very well in terms of positive funding changes. This is, of course, a matter of judgment, but if one believes that constant dollar changes over four percent per year are healthy, then one cannot help but conclude that R&D in the U.S. has been in a state of good health over the last ten years.

Note that one can only see from this type of pictorial display that the annual increases represented by double arrows are greater than four percent. The 1980 to 1984 period was somewhat stronger than the previous five year period in that the average annual rate of increase was 5.2 percent, as compared to four and a half percent during the earlier period. One has to remember that this was driven heavily by the increases in federal defense funding. This helps to understand why the third row from the bottom of Chart 10 shows that industrial R&D performance has been very strong and that the national development effort which is depicted just above that row, has been strong almost all the way across this period.

One can also observe that for the federal contribution to the national R&D effort, the increases during the second half of the period have been a little bit more than they were during the first half. The one exception is in basic research, where the annual changes during the recent five year period have been somewhat lower than they were during the first half. However, basic research funding changes during the last five years still averaged of the order of almost two to three percent this year. In the applied area, the horizontal arrow under the federal government for the 1980-84 period shows that this funding has been leveling off. However, since industry changes in applied research funding (as shown in the next two columns) have been very strong, the overall effort has also been strong.

As for sectoral R&D performance, which is represented by the bottom three rows, industry has been in very good shape. Academia has had a little weaker experience in recent years and, relatively speaking federal intramural performance had the worst funding patterns.

Finally, let me show what this good R&D picture means in terms of an international R&D perspective. How do we compare to other countries? Chart 11 depicts what Dr. Ross mentioned this morning. I picked 1982 as the year for comparison because it is the year for which we can get the latest data from other countries; we have more recent data from the United States. If one looks at 1982, the total United States R&D effort, as represented by R&D expenditures, is more -- not much more -- than the sum of the efforts of Japan, West Germany, France, and the United Kingdom. Thus, comparatively speaking, at least in the R&D area -- and I realize this is only one phase of the S&T process -- the United States still is the major power in the world.

How our relative status has changed over time can be seen from Chart 12, which normalizes the absolute magnitudes of R&D expenditures by dividing them by the respective gross national products (GNPs). The chart shows that during the sixties and almost up to the late seventies this ratio declined for the United States while in other countries such as Japan and West Germany it moved up. However, it is important to realize that since the end of the seventies the R&D/GNP ratios for the countries shown on the chart have increased in parallel. In other words, the catching up process seems to have stopped during the last ten years and all the countries seem to be putting more resources into R&D at about the same rate. Consequently, the United States position with respect to the other countries, has stayed essentially the same or even improved a bit during the last five years.

I should point out that the USSR seems to have a fairly flat R&D/GNP pattern now. I also should alert you that the data for the USSR are not nearly as good as those from the other countries. However, even within this relatively high level of uncertainty, USSR R&D does not seem to be increasing at the rate it did during the early part of the 1961-83 period.

Well, there you have it, an overview of what has been happening in terms of R&D funding during the last ten years. I hope that this information will be of utility during the rest of this conference and stimulate a healthy discussion of what all of this means, of the causal factors for these funding patterns, and of what the future might hold in store. I believe that a factual

41

overview such as the one I have presented might be a good starting point for all of your future conferences. It certainly should prevent a lot of arguments during the discussion whether something is bigger or smaller and it might stimulate new ideas and discussion thrusts.

THE NATIONAL R&D EFFORT
1984 — $97.9 BILLION

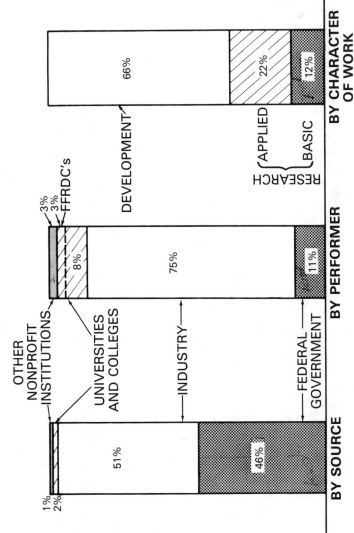

BY SOURCE

OTHER NONPROFIT INSTITUTIONS
UNIVERSITIES AND COLLEGES
INDUSTRY
FEDERAL GOVERNMENT

1%
2%
51%
46%

BY PERFORMER

FFRDC's
3%
3%
8%
75%
11%

BY CHARACTER OF WORK

DEVELOPMENT
66%
APPLIED 22%
BASIC 12%
RESEARCH

SRS 84-607

SOURCE: NATIONAL SCIENCE FOUNDATION

Federal R&D Funding by Selected Function

(1972 Constant Dollars)

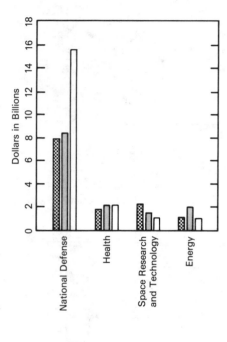

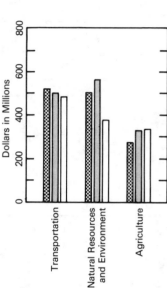

1975
1980
1985

Source: Division of Science Resources Studies/STIA.

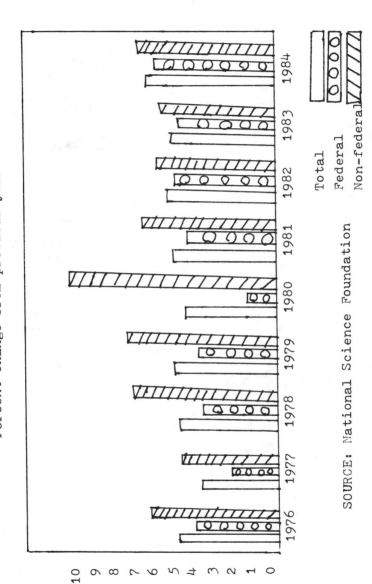

NATIONAL R&D EXPENDITURES (1972 Constant Dollars)
Percent change from previous year

Total
Federal
Non-federal

SOURCE: National Science Foundation

CHART 3

National Expenditures for Development by Source

(1972 Constant Dollars)

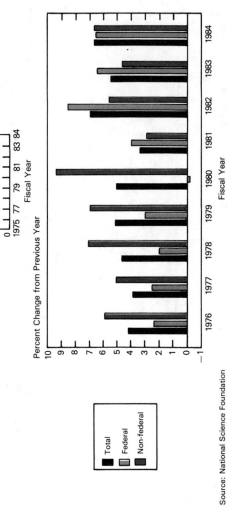

Percent Change from Previous Year

Fiscal Year

Total
Federal
Non-federal

Source: National Science Foundation

National Expenditures for Applied Research by Source

(1972 Constant Dollars)

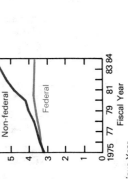

Dollars in Billions

Total

Non-federal

Federal

Fiscal Year

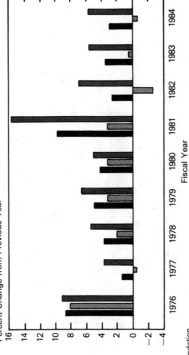

Percent Change from Previous Year

Fiscal Year

Total
Federal
Non-federal

Source: National Science Foundation

National
Expenditures for
Basic Research
by Source

(1972 Constant Dollars)

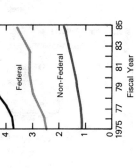

Dollars in Billions

Total

Federal

Non-Federal

Fiscal Year

Percent Change from Previous Year

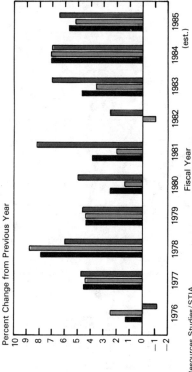

Total
Federal
Non-federal

Fiscal Year

Source: Division of Science Resources Studies/STIA.

Federal R&D
Expenditures
by Performer
(1972 Constant Dollars)

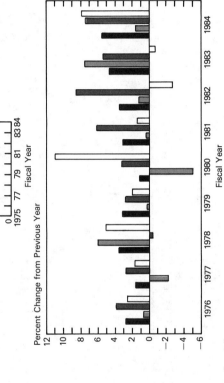

Dollars in Billions

Total

Industrial
Firms

Federal
Intramural

Universities
and Colleges

Fiscal Year

Percent Change from Previous Year

Fiscal Year

Total
Federal
Intramural
Industrial
Firms
Universities
and Colleges

Source: National Science Foundation

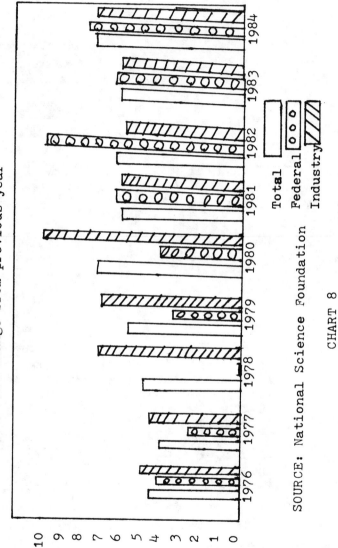

INDUSTRIAL R&D EXPENDITURES BY SOURCE
(1972 Constant Dollars)

Percent change from previous year

Total
Federal
Industry

SOURCE: National Science Foundation

CHART 8

Academic R&D Expenditures by Source

(1972 Constant Dollars)

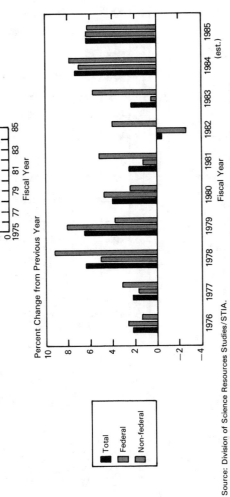

Dollars in Billions

Total

Federal

Non-Federal

Fiscal Year

1975 77 79 81 83 85

Percent Change from Previous Year

Total
Federal
Non-federal

Fiscal Year

1976 1977 1978 1979 1980 1981 1982 1983 1984 1985 (est.)

Source: Division of Science Resources Studies/STIA.

Changes in R&D Expenditure Patterns

Source / Performance	Federal 1975-79	Federal 1980-84	Private 1975-79	Private 1980-84	Total 1975-79	Total 1980-84
National R&D						
Basic Research						
Applied Research						
Development						
Industrial R&D Performance						
Academic R&D Performance						
Federal R&D Performance						

Symbol — Average Annual Rate of Change

- > 4%
- 1-4%
- ± 1%

Source: National Science Foundation

International R&D
Expenditures: 1982

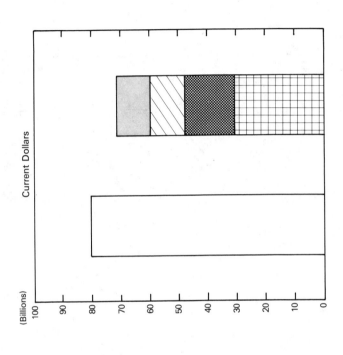

Current Dollars

(Billions)

100 90 80 70 60 50 40 30 20 10 0

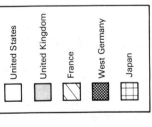

- [ ] United States
- [▨] United Kingdom
- [▨] France
- [▨] West Germany
- [▨] Japan

INTERNATIONAL R&D EXPENDITURES AS PERCENT OF GNP

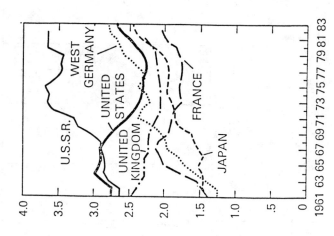

- THE U.S. DEVOTES HIGHER PROPORTION OF ECONOMY TO R&D THAN MOST COUNTRIES EXCEPT THE U.S.S.R. AND WEST GERMANY.

SOURCE: DIVISION OF SCIENCE RESOURCES STUDIES/STIA

DISCUSSION

MR. HOGAN: Thank you, Charlie. I am sure all of us here are pleased to see most of the lines heading certainly in the right direction. From every indication that we have, 1985 suggests that it will be a continuation of what we have had in the recent past. We have time for just a couple of questions, so please come to the microphone.

DR. ZAHRT: Ken Zahrt from Dayton, Ohio. I have one question on your figures. How did you treat independent research and development in the government contracts? Did you allocate that to industry or as a government expenditure?

DR. FALK: While most independent R&D is included, we are not sure where it is since different companies have different reporting practices. From our discussions with responding officials we know that most companies report it as a company expenditure. However, this ambiguity does not cause a serious distortion of the data since IR&D is only about three to four billion dollars. However, not all R&D type of funds are included.

DR. ZAHRT: I would think with increasing defense dollars being spent and a percentage of each contract going toward applied research of the contractor's choice with government oversight, that would be becoming a substantial amount.

DR. FALK: It certainly will increase, but as I pointed out it represents only about five percent of industrial R&D expenditures. With respect on how to report it, these are different points of view. Many companies feel that IR&D dollars are their own, not government funds. The rationale is that they receive this money from the government for their own R&D use. Some of the government agencies have a somewhat different view. Certainly, I believe that these funds should be considered as government funds, since after all, the government does provide the companies with funds for some of this R&D type of activity.

DR. ZAHRT: Some of industry did report it as research, their own expenditures?

DR. FALK: When we talked to them about it, many say that they include it as part of their funds.

DR. ZAHRT: You are making the flat statement that it is not included.

DR. FALK: I think it generally is not. Tom Hogan is responsible for the collection of the data and he might want to

43

comment.

MR. HOGAN: It is an area that is still very fuzzy as far as the collection of data is concerned. What we do, in the industry sector, as we do in the other sector, too, but specifically speaking about industry, we provide companies with definitions, specific definitions of what research and development are.

Then within that, they work to determine how much of their IR&D budget really fits within those specifications.

Unfortunately, as best we are able to determine at the moment, there is not any uniform agreement at all as to how much of these funds should really be included, how much of bid and proposal costs should be included. That generally says it. We are working to see what we can do to try to clarify and make our definitions in this area a little bit tigher.

DR. YOUNG: I am Leo Young, with OSD in DOD. I have responsibility for IR&D. For '84 IR&D totals about five billion dollars, of which roughly one-third comes from the Defense Department, one-third from other government agencies and other customers, and one-third from industry. This does not include the B&P, the bid and proposal, which is in addition.

DR. FALK: But as you can see, that is still the order of less than ten percent of the total.

MR. HOGAN: And also not all that is allowed. Isn't that true, Leo?

DR. YOUNG: Well, I can go into a lot more detail.

MR. HOGAN: Just basically.

DR. YOUNG: The IR&D is negotiated between DOD and NASA and the corporations and the numbers I've given are the total indirect costs the companies expend on their own independent R&D, of which roughly one-third is paid for by DOD.

MR. HOGAN: Thank you.

DR. COOPER: Martin Cooper from Rohrback Technology. The question I would like to ask has to do with the working smarter, not harder issue. Moneys for R&D have generally been increasing, as your numbers show. Even now we are still ahead of most foreign countries, but the question is can we use the resources we have in a smarter way?

In particular, I know there have been attempts and I would like to know what is the latest in coming to grips with the issue of R&D productivity and can we focus resources better to really meet the competitive challenge?

DR. FALK: As I tried to point out in the beginning, some things can be measured more easily than others. I have discussed primarily inputs to the R&D process. It is much more difficult to measure the outputs and even more difficult to deal with a meaningful comparison of inputs and outputs, namely R&D productivity -- and I presume you mean how much new information is being turned out -- per unit of cost or effort. There is an equally important aspect, namely impact, that is how well that information is being used. One can have a very effective R&D system and yet from a point of view of national welfare have very little results. There are some countries that are good examples of exactly that situation. We at this conference must keep in mind that R&D is only one phase of the whole innovation process. That process involves at the beginning the creation of new knowledge, generally through R&D, then the transformation of this new knowledge into new products and processes and finally the diffusion and use of these products and processes. All phases of this phenomenon should be measured and then one could address objectively matters such as R&D productivity. We have developed some partial measures of inputs, outputs and impacts. Yet the art of measuring the latter two aspects, including R&D productivity, is still in its infancy. However, one can also address these issues without the benefit of quantitative measures. Hopefully this conference will focus on them because government policy has had an effect on them and is going to continue to influence how rapidly our R&D generated information is being translated into new products and processes.

DR. GLAZE: Bob Glaze from the University of Alabama in Birmingham. In your last slide you indicated the rate of increase of R&D expenditures as percentage of GNP for most of the major western industrial nations seemed to be fairly parallel at rate of increase.

With the great increase in military spending and the R&D component in the last four years, how much of the U.S. increase can be attributed to military spending and is that increase paralleled by military spending in the other countries?

DR. FALK: That is a very good point. As I pointed out, about two-thirds of the recent federal R&D expenditure increases were due to military spending. Indeed the international comparisons are quite different when one excludes defense R&D from the picture. Under these circumstances, West Germany and Japan have higher "civilian R&D expenditure to GNP" ratios than the U.S.; their ratios are about 2.45 in 1982 as compared to a U.S. ratio of about 1.8. However, there is a good reason for this since these countries put practically all their R&D resources into

45

civilian R&D spending.

DR. GLAZE: What about the rate of increase in the U.S., the slope of the curve, if you take it out?

DR. FALK: The slope of the U.S. civilian R&D/GNP curve has generally been upward, though it dropped between 1982 and 1983. However, one has to be careful on how to interpret this, since this ratio is a function of both the numerator (R&D expenditures) and the denominator (GNP). Thus it really indicates how one behaves relative to the other. In absolute terms, federal civilian R&D obligations, that is total minus defense, has been pretty flat from 1979 to 1984, at around 15 billion current dollars. However, in constant dollar terms it has declined by about 25 percent during this period.

MR. HOGAN: Thank you again, Charlie.

The next event on the program, as you will note, is really our first other than an overall general session, and this will be devoted to a commentary on the part of two very excellent spokesmen with regard to what the administration policy has been toward R&D during the past four years.

CHAPTER FOUR
"Administration Policy"

Dr. James Ling
Office of Science and Technology Policy

Introductory Remarks

DR. HOLMFELD: One of the temptations for all of us who work in this area of federal science policy is to say to ourselves that the time for a major review, for new directions, is at hand and let us look at that.

Many times we are probably wrong and we are probably exaggerating our own importance. Let me suggest, however, to you that at this time there are a number of indications that a watershed in federal science policy may be at hand, to quote a more prominent member of the government.

There are an unusual number of studies going on in the field of science policy. You heard this morning Dr. Ross mention the administration's study of international competitiveness.

In addition to that, we have had or we are about to have two, I think, important and major studies coming out of panels from the White House Science Council. We had the Packard Report on the federal labs within the last six months.

We are about to get early next year another Packard Panel Report, the Panel on University Research and University Science Training. That panel is meeting now and I think will have an important impact.

There is also, as I understand it, a study going on by the Industrial Research Institute of whether or not they can do more to take advantage of and utilize the results of federal research. That group is also at work now. I do not know exactly when they expect to report, but I think a lot of people are looking forward to what they may have to say.

And then there is a study in the Congress which will begin next January. The House of Representatives Science and Technology Committee is about to initiate what we hope will be a careful and in depth review of federal science policy.

Another small indication, I think, of the importance and concern about federal science policy appeared last night when one of the candidates several times referred to the importance of advancing science and the federal government's role in that.

The study that I am associated with -- I will just very briefly mention it -- is limited to science. It will not deal with technology policy. That is mainly because we think that both science and technology policy are too big an area to cover.

But technology policy has undergone a major change. Charlie Falk referred to the numbers. One way of describing it is to describe what happens when a group of supply side economists get together in the room and the light bulb burns out. What do they do about it? The answer is nothing; they wait for the invisible hand to change the light bulb.

In science policy there has been a similar dramatic change. Dr. Ross mentioned Dr. Keyworth's talk to the American Asssociation for the Advancement of Science (AAAS) last year. Many in this room will remember Dr. Keyworth's talk to the AAAS in 1981 when he stated unequivocally that science expenditures by the federal government, like any other expenditure, would have to take its lumps when it came to cutting the federal deficit.

That is no longer the case. And as we saw from the numbers, the Science Office and the White House have made a substantial change in that policy. And while they do not support technology development in the civilian sector, they are giving strong support to civilian science expenditures, including expenditures for university research.

One final indication of the change that I think we are about to see in this area is the attitude by some members of Congress towards federal research expenditures.

Most people here will have read about disputes and discussions that have taken place in the last year and a half when amendments were offered on the floor of the House of Representatives to influence through the political process the expenditure of federal funds for science.

About three weeks ago my boss, Congressman Fuqua, received a letter signed by a number of prominent science administrators, headed by Dr. Keyworth, in which it was urged that practice be suppressed, if that is the right word, or certainly not be followed in the future.

Chairman Fuqua's answer was a change represents a change. He indicated that science, when it comes to decisions about science at the individual project level, it is clear that scientific judgments, that is, the peer review process, must and probably should continue to predominate.

When it comes to expenditures and investment of the taxpayer's money for major facilites which affect such things as regional

48

economic development, then that process of peer review cannot be the only one. It should probably continue to play a substantial factor, but other factors, including concern about economic development and other kinds of factors that come into the political process can, should and will undoubtedly play a role.

This means a number of things, but it means more than anything else that science has entered the big leagues. One of the things that I hope you will be able to discuss at this conference is what that means. I do not think the process where science is small potatoes, an Ivory Tower activity totally isolated from the political process, will continue.

I think there are an increasing number of members who realize not only is this important for their own districts, but clear, unequivocal importance for the country. Therefore, we will see more interest in science, more interest in science expenditures and, undoubtedly, both good and bad effects arising from that.

Well, I have tried to suggest to you a number of factors which suggest a time of substantial change. To tell us more about that and give us an indepth perspective, we are very fortunate to have with us James Ling from the White House Office of Science and Technology Policy (OSTP).

Jim has been with OSTP since this administration began. He obtained his bachelor's degree in chemistry, has two master's degrees in nuclear and industrial engineering and has a PhD in an interdisciplinary field which covers operational research, nuclear engineering and industrial engineering.

Prior to his coming to OSTP, he served with the Department of Energy for three years, for the MITRE Corporation for three years, with the DuPont Company in a research capacity in the field of energy and nuclear energy, and with the United States Air Force for over 20 years.

DR. LING

Thank you very much, John. I cannot resist the observation that maybe science has entered the big leagues, but some of us wonder if it has not entered the pork barrel, and I think that may be of greater concern to us over there on the White House Staff.

Anyway, as we approach the end of the first term of this administration, it is certainly timely to look back over the past three and a half years to see what science and technology policy has been and how it has been implemented.

49

I would like to review that policy with you and look at some specific examples of implementation. So, basically what I am going to try to do today is say what was the philosophy underlying the science policy, what has been the science policy and has the administration really followed through on that. In other words, have the things that have been done been consistent with the policy.

First of all, this administration came into office with a very strong commitment to science and technology. Early on it stated its intention to develop and implement a new science and technology policy, one that was developed not so much in response to the needs of the science community, but which was in response to the broader needs of the nation.

That is what Jay Keyworth said when he first came in and that apparently bothered some people. But there it is, the science policy is to support the national needs rather than the needs of the science community. To the extent those two needs are congruent, that is fine, but the national need should be dominant.

The administration articulated a policy that linked science and technology to overall national goals. I would like to reemphasize that because from our perspective there was a tendency in the past to look at growth in R&D expenditures as an end in itself rather than consider what it was contributing to the overall good of the country.

From the outset the administration has said that maintaining and increasing the nation's science and technology capability are critical to realizing two of its major national goals, a revitalized economy and a restored defense posture.

As the economic climate has improved, the emphasis has shifted from revitalizing the economy to sustaining economic growth and particularly improving US industrial competitiveness in the world market.

Let me give you a little bit of an historical perspective so perhaps you understand some of the philosophical underpinnings of the science policy. You have already seen this morning that we are certainly number one in the world in terms of capability to perform R&D. How did that come about? Primarily it goes back to World War II, to the tremendous investments made by the federal government, the building up of institutions in the form of federal laboratories, in the form of great research universities, and this growth was very strong certainly through the 50's and the 60's.

It began to taper off a little bit in the 70's, but now in the

50

80's, as we look around us, the world is very different. We are in a very different environment from that which existed immediately after World War II and probably through the mid 60's. For one thing, we are no longer the unchallenged giant among R&D performers in the world. We have competition.

The other thing is that our resources are strained to the point where we are not able to do all the things we would like to do. I think growth for its own sake, which was perhaps a worthy goal in the 50's and 60's, may no longer be applicable.

So one of the things we have to ask ourselves is: what do we do with this tremendous investment; are we getting an adequate return for this investment in R&D as a nation and how should we make the institutions, the performers of R&D, work better? That is, as Ian Ross has already referred to this morning, how do we create a new synergism among major performers; that is industry, universities and the federal government? That forms the background of the administration's policy regarding science and technology.

Now (with that in mind) since the beginning, the administration has applied three criteria to R&D funding by the federal government. These have been excellence and relevance and appropriateness.

I would like to describe each of these in a little more detail. Excellence means that we are clearly committed to supporting the best, whether it is people or ideas or institutions. History has certainly proven that success in science and in technology has gone to those who have been uncompromising in their striving for excellence. We believe that excellence breeds excellence and that if the emphasis is on quality first, then quantity will eventually take care of itself.

For example, if we support the best professor we can find in a certain field, then we need not worry about how many graduate students are going to follow along. The graduate students will, in their own search for excellence, seek out that professor. So, quality and not quantity, we believe, is what provides leadership.

DISCUSSION

DR. STEVENSON: Jim Stevenson from Georgia Tech. About four or five years ago we were visited by our National Advisory Board and they recommeneded that our ratio of industrial research, the government research, should really be about 50/50. That sort of startled all of us, but since that time we have increased from about ten to 20.

The question I have, I guess, is in the policies that the federal government is looking at. What is your feeling about that ratio?

DR. LING: We have not come up with any specific ratio. We feel that there should be more industry involvement.

I think we share the concern that some of the universities have expressed, that they see a danger in getting too heavily involved with industry because of the generally applied nature. In other words, they do not want to be R&D captive contractors to industry and they feel the federal grants tend to give them more autonomy.

I guess I would agree with that. Fifty/fifty might be a bit high. I think it depends on the individual university. I would not want to define a specific level, but I would say that the potential danger of ending up as an industrial R&D contractor needs to be balanced off against the need for university autonomy and the need to pursue new ideas.

DR. STEVENSON: And how about the foreign influence, foreign industry, in American universities?

DR. LING: I do not know how widespread that is. Obviously we have a concern. If we are talking about industrial competitiveness, the last thing we want is for our good ideas to be exported. We feel that we ought to take care of Amercia first.

I think again, rather than have the federal government dictate some sort of policy, I think that is something which each university needs to be aware of and sort of consider what they are doing within the overall national context. And if that means being cozier with Ford than with Toyota, so be it. I would leave that to the individual conscience, at least at this point.

DR. WAKS: As you know, I am Norm Waks of the Mitre Corporation. I believe we are talking about an R&D program, national R&D program, that is now nearly 100 billion dollars. I wanted to ask kind of a question at a level somewhat, it seems to

52

me, above the level of the talk you actually gave, if I could.

And to put it in perspective, let me say last year we were quite interested in learning what the administration's R&D policy program was in the broad -- it had had four or five basic tenents -- and what the administration hoped to accomplish by what were really some fundamental changes in science and technology policy and get an interim progress report.

This year, some of us at least, hoped what we could get would be at the end of the administration's term or first term, depending on the outcome of the elections, was what I would charactize as a report card (both from somebody from the administration and somebody from the Congress) in an overall sense on those basic policies as it affects this whole 100 billion dollard national R&D juggernaut.

Let me ask a couple of questions so you know what I mean by report card. First, is the administration satisfied that its new policies are being carried out?

Two, does the administration know what the effects of these new policies are, satisfied that it knows, on the various R&D performing sectors who are here?

Third, is the administration satisfied with these effects if it knows them, and the same kind of thing I would hope would come from somebody on the congressional side with a broad national perspective.

I wonder if you could give us a feel for a report card at that level on the big part of it, not the initiatives and the funding and things like that, which we have readily available to us.

DR. LING: Well, I think I tried to get across the idea that I think we feel that there have been results. Some of these, as I point out, are hard to quantify. It is easy to quantify the funding and again because of the time lag, if you think back to the charts that Charlie Falk had, the real impact at universities, for example, is only now beginning to show up.

By talking to people, we get a feeling that things are happening out there. And again I would appeal to a group like this, in the course of your discussions, to confirm or reject that notion if you feel that it isn't happening.

DR. WAKS: Jim, that is exactly my point. As a setting for that and the panels after this, are you satisfied, speaking for the administration, that these policies are being carried out and that you know what the effects are and that you are satisfied with them? It is to get your perspective.

DR. LING: Our perspective is we are encouraged. We are not omniscient, but the feedback we have shows that no flags of disaster have been raised on this point, and I think the encouraging thing is that we hear a lot of people saying the same things that we are. Hopefully that is genuine and they are not just trying to make us feel good.

As I say, when you pick up a university publication and you read words like, "search for excellence, investment in excellence, build talent, cooperate with industry, revitalize the economy, improve industrial competitiveness," you at least get the sense there is an echo coming back. So at this point that is about the best we can do.

DR. WAKS: In summing up then, would it be unfair to ask you to verify the following statements: The administration is satified with these policies and intends to continue them?

DR. LING: Yes.

DR. BARKER: Robert Barker from Cornell University. I would like to ask a question about an area that has not been addressed, and that is facilities. I guess it was referred to as pork barrel, but it seems to be an area in which we do not have a policy. What I would like to ask is whether you see us developing one and if so, how?

DR. LING: I think that is going to be an item of major concern in the next administration, next term, because clearly enough questions have been raised on this issue.

We need to go back, and we have in some instances gone back and looked at what the government did in the fifties and sixties, going back to this period, when a lot of these places were established, and see what it was we did then and whether those same kinds of approaches are applicable now or if something else needs to be done. I think we are totally sympathetic to the problem of decaying buildings, in addition to the obsolescence of equipment and so forth.

By the way, one of the purposes of this university study, which was also mentioned, that our office is doing, which will come out probably in the next couple of months, is to focus on that very issue. The basic question is: is there a special relationship between the federal government and the universities or are universities simply another purveyor of R&D? I think the answer to the last point is clearly no. There is a special relationship.

Then if you say yes, there is a special relationship, what

does that lead to and does it lead to a government obligation to do certain things for and with the universities? I think that is one of the things that is going to come out of the study.

DR. BARKER: Do you have any suggestions about how the universities might function differently with respect to relationships with elements in the federal government to better assist them in the development of priorities or initiatives in areas like this one?

It seems to me some communities, like the physics community, in my view, has a pretty means of putting in front of the federal government what its options should be, with regard to same, i.e., good physics.

I do not see a similar mechanism working for the universities in perhaps what is nationally a more important area, the rebuilding of the universities infrastructure for basic research and for doing the interactions, which I am very much in favor of, between university and industry.

DR. LING: I think the National Academy of Sciences has this University-Government Forum, which I think was established to do exactly that. And I think there is someone here who is probably more familiar with it.

DR. PHILLIPS: Don Phillips with the Government-University-Industry Research Round Table. Actually my question was about another sector which seems to be important in talking about the restructuring of the American science policy or American scientific enterprise. We will hear one example of this sector tomorrow, and that is state government.

I make the hypothesis that what has been going on in the states (to some extent through investments of significant sums of money -- through a center similar to what is being proposed here in Virginia -- and to some extent not by money, but by trying to catalyze or stimulate various types of activity) has been generally decoupled from what is being talked about and considered at the federal level.

As you think about the future, both in this and the next administration, and through reanalysis of American science policy, how do you think the initiatives and thinking going on at the state level should or could be better, coupled with the federal level.

DR. LING: I think we are certainly encouraged by what we see at the state level and I think we are certainly encouraging the federal agencies to work with the states.

For example, I alluded to the new research institutes. We have one up in Maryland, in which it was the county that actually donated the land for a new biological research insitute, with participation by the National Bureau of Standards, University of Maryland, NIH, and I believe even the Department of Agriculture is involved, plus industry.

So I think that is really the kind of thing we would like to see. I will say I guess we have not really gone out and beaten bushes in the states as much, but we certainly have applauded such efforts and have not stood in the way of anything like this that has come along.

Certainly I think it would be great if we had more, and we have been at least touting that example as one which I think should be emulated.

DR. HILL: Chris Hill, I am with the Congressional Research Service. A number of times in our nation's past, when we felt challenged by either problems or opportunities in the field of science and technology, we have chosen an institutional solution.

For World War II, the Office of Scientific Research and Development; in the fifties the Science Foundation; during the Sputnik era the reconstitution of NASA and establishment of a permanent Presidential Science Advisor mechanism; and in the early and again mid seventies the founding of ERDA and the Department of Energy.

Recognizing that this administration is not given to institutional solutions as its first thought, are you satisfied in OSTP that our current federal institutions are structured in a way that allows us to meet the challenge of international competitiveness, the need to revitalize a number of our industries, to be sure our growing industries remain growing and so on?

Do we have the right institutional mechanism? And the rumors I occasionally hear -- you might be thinking about new ones -- is there any truth to those?

DR. LING: I think what you have mentioned is certainly something which occupies a lot of our thought. I think we need to look at the problem in a little more detail and really up to this point, at least within the first term, there have been so many other things going on that I do not think that the question which you raise has been really uppermost in our minds.

It could well be in the second term. The study Congress is about to launch will also deal with this. So the topic is certainly a timely one and I am sure that you are going to hear

56

more about it.

CHAPTER FIVE
"Impacts on Industry"

Dr. Milton Stewart
Robbins and Green

Introductory Remarks

We now begin the first of three sessions devoted to examining the impact of the new federal policies on the individual sectors.

This afternoon Charles Larson, Executive Director of the Industrial Research Institute, has assembled an impressive group of speakers to look at these impacts. He will also tell us a little bit about some of the recent things that the IRI has been doing. Chuck.

MR. CHARLES LARSON: Thank you, Tom. We are going to talk about industrial research this afternoon, and we are going to cover three sectors. The first is small business, which is a very important aspect of industry and industrial research. There is a lot more small business than big business. We are also going to talk about big business and we are going to talk about the triad of industry, government and universities.

As I told my speakers at lunch, I am not aware of what they are going to say this afternoon. However, I am encouraged by the way things are going for industrial R&D and I believe that most signs are positive, as we saw this morning.

This was reflected recently by a report on R&D spending of 22 major industrial corporations during the first half of 1984. Their average increase in R&D for the first six months was 13.3 percent, with the pharmaceutical and electronic firms showing increases of 30 percent or more. IBM, for example, spent over 1.9 billion dollars from January to June this year. That is nearly 15 million dollars every working day, which is more than most countries even spend on R&D.

Now, no company has ever spent more than three billion dollars in one year on R&D, but IBM is going to spend close to four billion dollars this year and that is up significantly from the two and a half billion dollars they spent last year.

Surveys show that industry spent some 44 billion dollars on R&D in 1983. It is expected to rise to 48 billion dollars this year and probably 53 billion dollars in 1985.

It is interesting to note that just four companies, IBM, GM, AT&T and Ford, will account for about one-quarter of this spending.

Industry, of course, is also a major employer of both scientists and engineers, with about 690,000 scientists or 46 percent of the total, and some 1,350,000 engineers, or about 75 percent of the total.

R&D activity engages about half of these scientists and about one-third of the engineers. Thus the total number of scientists and engineers in industrial R&D is close to 800,000 or about one-quarter of the total number in the United States.

Employment in this sector grew at a rate of six percent from 1972 through 1982, paused in 1983, and is growing again at about the same rate as before.

A recent trend survey of 100 member companies of the Industrial Research Institute indicated that 75 percent plan slightly or significantly higher R&D expenditures in 1985. Fifty-four percent plan to increase R&D professional employment slightly, with nine percent planning a significant increase.

Hiring of new graduates was only slightly less optimistic, with 39 percent planning a slight increase and nine percent planning a significant increase. Thirty-eight percent of them planned no change in the hiring of new graduates. Thus, I believe the job market for industrial R&D employment looks to be in good health.

An examination of the Republican and Democratic platforms shows no great difference in regard to industrial R&D, which is in sharp contrast to some of the other areas that we heard about last night. This is in large part because industrial policy has not emerged as a proposal by the Democrats.

The Democratic platform has a small section devoted exclusively to R&D, in which it is recommended that, "The U.S. should increase the percentage of GNP devoted to commercially related R&D as a long term spending goal."

It goes on to say, "As Democrats, our goal is to increase civilian R&D in this country, to expand its commerical application and to provide more industries with the opportunity to take advantage of it."

It goes on, "Because R&D, critical as it is for our growing high technology industry, is no less important for our basic industries ... the Democratic Party will encourage cooperation between states and the private sector in supporting technology development."

It notes that state development agencies are already seeking closer ties to both business and universities and that universities are looking to the private sector in setting their research agendas. Thus the Democratic party, "will encourage and support centers that provide for cooperation of academic and entrepreneurial excellence."

In a section labeled "Science and Technology" the Republican platform says, "We pledge to continue the Reagan Administration's science and technology policies," which we heard this morning. "We propose to extend incremental research and tax credit to stimulate greater activity in the private sector, and to allow U.S. firms to compete with foreign companies, we will permit U.S. firms to cooperate in joint R&D activities."

A week ago Thursday the House approved and sent to the President a bill that had already passed the Senate that would reduce the antitrust liability of certain R&D joint ventures by limiting the court awards to actual rather than triple damages in any private civil suit against joint R&D activity that is disclosed in advance to the Justice Department. This bill also bars courts from finding any action by joint R&D ventures illegal without considering whether it had pro-competitive effects that outweighed its anti-competitive effects.

These are things that I know Bruce Merrifield has been pushing hard for the last three years and I know he is delighted they are now virtually reality. The President is expected to sign this legislation, I believe, on October 11th.

The major challenge for industry now, as I view it, is the commercialization of new technology and we heard Ian Ross touch on that this morning. We have all the tools we need to compete and we are developing new tools every day, but we have to put those tools to work effectively in the market place. I am sure you are anxious to hear how our speakers feel about what I have said and about many other matters, so I will introduce our first speaker.

He is Milton Stewart, President of the Small Business-High Technology Institute. He is also very active in other activities. He is Editor-at-Large of Inc. Magazine, Counsel at Chapman, Duff & Paul in Washington and at Robbins and Green in Phoenix. He was formerly Chief Counsel for Advocacy in the U.S. Small Business Administration and was Counsel to the White House Conference on Small Business. He is a graduate of NYU with a master's from Columbia University School of Journalism and a J.D. from George Washington University School of Law. Milt is going to talk to us about "The Next Small Business Revolution, or Technology's Bush Leagues Grow Up."

DR. MILTON STEWART

I would like, if I may, to begin with a quick review of some facts about small business in our country. There are 14 million enterprises in this country that have 500 or fewer employees. They produce approximately 50 percent of the private sector jobs. They employ among them more people than all the large companies defined as the Fortune Large Thousand put together. They employed more people than all the levels of government put together.

And yet they have not constituted a significant force in our country on their own behalf or on behalf of policies that would benefit them in science and technology or in public policy more generally.

They have been, for example, far less effective in the making of public policy than universities, than large companies, than trade unions, than farm groups, than consumer groups and many others.

This is a reflection of the basic characteristic of this constituency. It is stiff-necked individually and stiff-necked when it is all together. So that if you get five small business people of any kind in a room together, you will get at least five differing opinions about most subjects.

That is a way of saying that what I have to say may not represent revealed wisdom on the part of all of my fellow small business people. I have been in and out of the federal establishment six times now. I have never stayed more than 30 months. Clearly, that is our mutual toleration level. But that goes back 45 years now and I think I know a little bit how our government works.

But if you go back to when I first knew about it, small business was just becoming an issue. One of my first recollections about it goes back to when I worked in the Senate for the Senate Small Business Committee and I heard a conversation between Senator Taft of Ohio who was a Republican, and Senator Murray, who was chairman of our committee and a Democrat. They were discussing some legislation which was on the floor, talking about a colleague who was orating on the floor about how much he loved small business.

We had just had a rather close vote on an issue involving small business and he had voted against it. And one of these senators said to the other, "Did you see how that so and so voted?" And the other one said, "Do not call him a so and so, he is very much in favor of small business, so much so that he will not rest until he makes it as small as it can be."

That is a feeling many small business people have when they hear other people from other American communities of opinion talk one way and act another.

They are, for example, a little crusty in their attitude towards the academic community. We have a long tradition of town and gown hostility in this country. It is by no means dead. You will find small business people who have even attitudes you would call close to "barbarous" towards universities and what goes on in them.

But I think you must know that small business has had and continues to have a chip on its shoulder as it looks at the people who are part of the American science establishment, defined as they define it.

For example, at least fifty times this morning, the phrase "industry-university cooperation" was used. That is code in Washington for big company-big university cooperation. That is what industry-university cooperation means in the federal agencies committed to supporting industry-university cooperation, something I emphatically support.

It was not always so in this country. Review the history of the growth of our land grant colleges and independent agricultural and independent education in this country. We came to be the world's agriculturally preeminent nation because of the long, strong tie between independent enterprise and independent education.

Two things have created a major problem for small companies. First, the rise in size of other institutions -- government, large companies, large universities. Second, the fact that these large institutions do business with one another according to terms and definitions, which until very recently have frozen small business pretty much out of the game.

Let me also go on record emphatically, before we get to really controversial matters, as being among those who are committed to the merit principle in science and in technology and in life itself. But "merit" has a way of turning into something else if those who are in charge of defining it are not clear about their own biases.

For example, I became interested in this subject matter really for about three reasons. You heard one labored at great length this morning, our world industrial competitiveness problem. I am not among those who are totally optimistic about it. I am far less optimistic about it than anyone you heard this morning.

62

Our country often deserves to be called the "five minutes of 12 country." Five minutes of 12 we get ready for war. Five minutes of 12 we deal with mass unemployment. Five minutes of 12 we deal with mass unemployment. Five minutes of 12 we deal with whatever national disasters we have to deal with. Sometimes we do not. Then it is five minutes after 12 and our institutions do not change rapidly enough to deal with the problems that are confronting them.

This is much on my mind today because I spent a good part of yesterday reading a report on Japanese venture businesses, small high technology companies in Japan. I have spent time in Japan. I have a high regard for Japanese society, for Japanese scientists and business people. And each time I have been there I have been astonished by my own blunders about their ability to use time.

What this report makes plain is that Japan is ten years ahead of where I thought they would be today in terms of the development of advanced small high technology companies. They function on industrial frontiers, taking basic science results and putting them to work in industry quickly, quickly, quickly.

When I first became interested in that problem it seemed surprising to me that with our long lead in the basic sciences with our adroit major corporations, I could not understand how we were surpassed in industry after industry. For the first time, we saw our companies whipped in our own home markets, not in one industry, two, five, ten, but in fifty. And I saw us lie to ourselves again and again and for years, first about whether it was really happening and then about why it was happening.

We kept boasting about our basic science advantages, about how many Nobel prize winners we were turning out. We never noticed the results of basic science were being put to work in other countries more rapidly than in our own.

There is now a systematic effort in Japan to bring small high technology companies into their science establishment. This is being done the way the Japanese do most things. After a concensus decision, arrived at after careful research, they know more about the contribution of American small high technology companies to science advance than most Ph.D.s in science in our country do.

All of this is a small reflection of a larger problem, but a very pertinent one. I have spent most of my life involved in the problems of these 14 million small enterprises because -- I am happy to say it here in Virginia -- I am a classic Jeffersonian in terms of outlook and I really believe that liberty and economic diversity go together and that hubris is not a uniquely Greek sin, but it is one every American is born with. We are taught as we grow up we are better than other people and we cannot help sometimes believing it.

I have often wished we had a sign in the office of every CEO in every major company and every agency head in Washington. It should carry that old slogan taught to slaves sent to ride with a conquering general returned for his triumphal march into Rome. You remember, as he rode into the city, a slave was put in his chariot to repeat: "Remember you are not a God."

When we came out of World War II we thought we were. We had the greatest industrial system in the world, the most productive science and technology apparatus, and long leads in every science and in every technology.

And I wish to express a resounding dissent to the general proposition that the reason we have lost ground since then is that we have not spent enough money. We have not spent money properly.

We do need to spend a higher share of our gross national product on science and technology, but unless we spend it on technology as well as science, unless we work at the links between basic science and applied technology, it will not matter how much we spend, we will continue to be outclassed in world industry.

Dollar for dollar, for example, if you invest in technology advance in a small business, you are likely to get a better return than if you spend it almost any other way. If you know about small business, research repeatedly confirming that will not surprise you. It has no vice-presidents of this, that, the other thing. It has a very few people working day and night to do as much as possible with as little as possible.

It heads for niches in the market place where it can survive. So that it self-selects critical places of need. And it knows that it cannot exist unless it does it cheaper or qualitatively better or both.

American small high technology companies must be accepted as full partners of the American science establishment as quickly and fully as possible. Unless that happens, it will not matter how much more money you spend in universities, large companies, and government labs.

We will get big ticket research and big ticket results for our research. Our blunders will simply match those of our rival the Soviet Union -- that is its game. While we are playing that game, all the other countries that have learned how to put their bets on small enterprises with low overhead and hard-driving people running them -- those nations will continue to mop up in the civilian market place.

The impact of government policies on the small business sector with respect to science and technology has, I believe it is fair to say, been symbolically favorable, yet really unfavorable.

This is Tom Hogan's study of small company procurement for NSF. In the private sector, firms under 500 employees spend about 3.8 percent of the R&D money in the country.

I computed the short fall as $250 million a year. What that says is that despite the gains we have made, small firms still do not share in the federal R&D dollars, even to the extent that they do in the private sector.

What are we talking about here? Out of these 14 million enterprises, we are talking about 13,000 small enterprises according to Census figures Tom relied on in his most recent report. It also resembles the figure the Treasury uses for the number of companies that qualified for the federal R&D tax credit, or tried to in the first year. In my view, that is far too small a number of companies for the future technology safety of our country.

We are not investing enough in or procuring enough from small high technology firms. There are not enough companies. They are not profitable enough. They are not well managed enough and so on and so forth. There has nevertheless been a net improvement in the outlook for them. What that reflects, first and foremost, the Federal Small Business Innovation Research Program. Moreover, the states are beginning to become interested. More and more people in large universities, government agencies, including government laboratories, are beginning to see and to acknowledge that there is benefit for them from a better working relationship with small high technology companies.

Unfortunately, that is true for a small number of basic science firms. There are small contractors who exist doing basic science research for large firms and for the government. Most of them operate on advanced technology problems which are too small for big companies to bother with or for big laboratories to bother with.

The Federal SBIR Program is, by far, the best federal procurement program ever devised for small business. It is not a program to help sick firms. It is not a program to help struggling small businesses, not at all.

It is a program to identify firms that are the best performers of their size in the country and to help them compete for work the country needs. In the first year of the SBIR program, 45 million dollars in federal grants was made available which is to be used for small business innovation research competitions.

Exempt from the computation of this percentage is money going to basic science. In other words, in computing the percentage, the agency may not include money being spent for basic science. That was a specific agreement that was reached during the congressional consideration of the legislation.

Second, this is a two-step grant process. At each step there is specific provision for a financial collaboration between small companies and universities and nonprofit institutions.

This is something which has, so far, been greeted with the largest yawn in the history of the American academic life. I do not think more than five universities in this country have yet acknowledged in a systematic way the existence of 100 to 500 million dollars of research money which could be available to them between now and 1988.

I hope somebody, lots of people, get angry and tells me my university is doing so. I would love to hear about it. We have been looking for you. Because we heard a lot of people in white coats -- we call them crybabies in white coats -- explain how anxious they were to do relevant, excellent applied research.

But my impression is that the number of proponents who have established relationships -- small business proponents is what they must be -- who have established relationships with universities is not very great. And the responsibility for that is a twofold thing.

Before I quit I will tell you that we hope to do something specific this next year about mending this particular problem and bringing about a greater collaboration between universities and small businesses.

Overseas the SBIR program has been called "a pearl of a program." A federal agency, one of the 12 I mentioned, publishes a printed solicitation. SBA publishes a quarterly calender and schedule of them.

The DOD's solicitation, for example, came out on about October 1st, 1984. The closing date for submissions is 31 January, 1985. There is a long laundry list of research topics in here -- any one of them sounds great. There is a one-paragraph explanation of each of them.

66

Proponents who are interested in making proposals must be "small businesses." That means they may not have more than 500 employees. They may have only one employee and sometimes do. To bring you up to date, in the first year of this program, 40 million dollars was awarded in 785 grants probably to about 500 companies.

Assume you are a small business person with high technology capability, a small business company, or a university person who knows about the program. You find in an agency's solicitation something within the area of your own expertise and you are interested in doing more research. There are instructions given in each solicitation document, descriptions of the process of granting and the basis of grants. Peer review is used to apply the standards normal for competitive selection on the basis of exellence. The sole difference is that the applicants must be small businesses.

You prepare your proposal in a truncated form compared to most federal proposals. It may not exceed 25 pages. An outline is given you and forms are given you. In general, it is made as easy as possible for people who do not have time and money to spend writing proposals, but may have great skill and be great at science and technology.

The program represents, I think, a serious and successful adjustment by big government to many of the special needs and characteristics of small business. For example, this is the first program in which if the small firm develops something patentable, it gets the right to the patent. If proprietary information goes into its proposal, it may be labeled as such and the government is required not to disclose it to others. These are things that are terribly important to small business people.

In general, the reason I am able to be optimistic begins with the fact that small business has been so hostile to government, so persuaded the government was "its enemy." This is the first significant government overture to the 13,000 small high technology companies among the 14 million total. It will take time for small business to believe it, but it reflects a genuine desire to work with them.

In the process itself, you get three or four months to prepare and submit your proposal of 25 pages or less. It is reviewed by agency scientists and engineers. They may or not use peer review, but probably do. Each agency makes its own decision after the proposals have been scored.

Scoring involves factors we would all accept: technically most promising, how advanced and relevant scientifically, greatest demonstration of research competence on the part of proponents.

One element in all proposals is civilian market place application. Congress wrote into the law setting the program up a requirement that wherever possible there be a civilian technology application of the results of SBIR research. Now, clearly much of what the Defense Department funds has no initial applicability outside the defense area. But the fact that the proposor and DOD must think about it will create more applications than there would otherwise be. The process leads to the choice of a winner of what is called a Phase I award, all of $40,000 to $50,000.

It is a grant which you must use within six months to do a study of the "feasibility" of your proposal's producing a research result responsive to the government's statement of need. You write your report. If your proposal was a bummer and it does not work, you report and and that is the end of the process.

If, on the other hand, the results are encouraging and it appears that the line of technology approach you have suggested will work out, you are encouraged to submit a Phase 2 proposal. This one is for the full dress research project. It may take up to two years and its cost may run, the federal share of it, up to $500,000, a lot of money for a small company.

At the time you put your Phase 2 proposal in, you are also encouraged -- and the competitive situation makes this almost a requirement -- you are encouraged to bring in evidence that there is a private source of financing for a Phase 3, after the government's three, four or $500,000 Phase 2 dollars are spent.

The Phase 3 "contingent commitment," as it is called, preferably must come from someone in the private sector: a venture capital company, a bank, a large company, a group of wealthy individuals. Some groups in the market place say they have reviewed your proposal, have looked at you hard, and are prepared to say they will back you after the government's Phase 2 if only two things happen -- the government puts up the amount of money sought and the Phase 2 research produces the technical results sought. "If those two things happen, we have already agreed with the applicant on the terms and conditions of an investment or a loan -- it may be either or a combination of both -- for Phast 3 development which will take this process or product into the market place."

That is a letter that is usually sent in with the Phase 2 application. If it isn't, the agency may say: "it looks to us like you have a shot at Phase 2, but because we have so many good proposals that we can fund, your chances will be better if you can find a Phase 3 commitment."

Judging whether this whole program has succeeded or failed depends on who you are and what your interests are. Some people simply think this is money down a sewer. They have said so, some of them quite recently.

These are also people who know little or nothing about this program -- I happen to know that -- and care nothing about it. They have it in their heads that this program "takes money away from basic science, or universities, money we cannot get for basic science and university that is going off in this other terrible direction." These are people who regrettably have a short-sighted view of how decision making is done in this country. We have our own form of the Japanese consensus.

If the small business community in this country decides the future of science and technology in this country is not going to involve it, it will play a role in the making of decisions about how large that effort is going to be. And I will just as directly as I can simply tell you that unless funds brought into the science and technology parts of the budget clearly involve both the discovery of new knowledge and its application, whether in the market place or the defense establishment, the support for it will be far less than if it does.

There are people, as I say, who consider that this program cannot possibly succeed. Why? Whoever heard of Nobel prizewinners in small businesses. Well, believe it or not, I have. There are now six, I am told, and the number is going up.

Then university administrators put another hat on and say "this is terrible, who's going to teach the students? Maybe research people won't continue to accept the kind of salaries we offer them. They will make more money, they will make too much money, they will make more money than I do -- if, that is, they get.

A lot of pretty strange things have been said to me to "explain" why this program's approach is not supposed to be good for universities. I happen to think that it is perhaps the heart of the long-range solution of the relationship between universities and the business community.

People in small business are not what they were. Most of them have earned one or more academic degrees. They send their kids to schools and graduate schools. They contribute as alumni. They sit on boards of trustees. The town-gown thing is largely now a problem in the minds of a very small number of people on both sides. And we have to make sure those people do not upset the prospect of a very fruitful collaboration which is set out prospectively in this program.

For me this program is a regrettably short term experiment, far too short. It only is there until 1988. Congress will review it in 1987. If you know the innovation process -- I come out of the venture capital business and I ought to know -- seven to ten years is the normal time frame for an industrial innovation.

Many people in business, industry and government understand the competitive pressures we are under with respect to specific industry and products and processes. But, they have yet to understand that what is really being challenged is our industrial innovation process itself.

The whole thing, from basic science laboratories work, right out to peddling in the market place, it is that process that is under attack. It is challenged by people who are doing it differently in other countries. They may even use pieces of our process better than we do at the moment.

The national stake in making this particular program successful is high -- and I have no exaggerated notion, believe me, as to how much small business can do by itself. What is critical is how much small business can do with its other partners in this process. Universities, large companies, government laboratories, independent professionals, the financial community, all of them in our magnificently diverse society, are involved in the innovation process.

Unfortunately it is like many other things in our wonderful country. It is a disorderly process and it is not easy to get everybody moving in the same direction to the same drum beat. By definition we do not want that anyway, but we should at least all be moving generally in the same direction with respect to innovation.

We have gone to the trouble of organizing a Small Business High Technology Institute as a nonprofit institution. Its commitment is to work with all of the other elements in the innovation process as hard as it can to make this program succcssful. And then on the basis of its success, to generalize that success to a more productive role, not just small companies, but for small companies and each of the other elements of the innovation process.

DISCUSSION

DR. STEVENSON: Jim Stevenson, Georgia Tech. My experience, I guess, with this program is that it tends to structure the advancement of the small business too much and that basically you run into a stitution where a person in Phase 3 wants to run ahead to Phase 3 and it is very difficult.

DR. STEWART: From time to time that is a problem. On the other hand, I think it is a great coup when a small company is able to jump directly from Phase 1 to Phase 3 because a large company has heard about what they are doing and says "you do not need Phase 2, we will fund you." This does happen. It matters less, I think, how we get there than that we do get there.

DR. COOPER: My name is Martin Cooper. I am with Rohrback Technology. It is a small company. We are looking for technical ideas to develop and help businesses to grow. One of the problems I have not heard addressed either from the government people or from the university people that seems to be a particular burden on small businesses is something money cannot buy and that is _time_.

Six months to a university, six months to a General Electric or General Motors, they can handle that, but it has been our experience if we look at any idea and we cannot get somebody to work on it, we cannot afford six months and we just will not walk on to the next one. What can be done to accelerate that whole process in time?

DR. STEWART: This is a very bitter issue within this program. The best thing that has happened is that the State of New York has just enacted a piece of legislation which provides for matching grants for every New York company that wins a Phase 1 SBIR award. The timing of the state grant is designed to bridge the cash flow gap between Phase 1 and Phase 2. That is one way to do it and frankly we hope the other states will do the same thing.

Our institute did a state by state study and sent it to every governor. The governor of New York felt that his state ought to be doing a lot better than it was doing. He felt that in New York perhaps $100,000 up front would attract better companies and make help to lick the cash flow gap problem you heard about. That's why the state went into this matching grant effort. The first half million in matching funds has already been appropriated.

For a second good move to lick the cash flow gap, we must give credit to many of the federal people. Some federal agencies are

71

shortening the "no cash flow" time span between Phase 1 and Phase 2. They need to be sure, however, that the review process also has enough time.

DR. LANGENBERG: Don Langenberg, University of Illinois at Chicago. No questions, but three brief comments. Lest anybody get the idea this program is a brand new program, I think some recognition should be given to the fact that NSF, as far ago as '77, '78 --

DR. STEWART: Five years before the rest of government.

DR. LANGENBERG: -- really piloted the concept. Second comment, I am not sure the connection between the small businesses operating with SBIR grants and universities is as weak as you might have suggested.

I do not know what it is like in the first year of the expanded program, but as I recall, a study NSF did about two or three years ago on its own SBIR programs showed about half the SBIR small businesses had a university scientist or sometimes several associated with that project in some way, either as a consultant, as a principal in a small business or whatever.

The third comment I wanted to make is that for those of us in the university sector who have an interest in some involvement with technology, that part that might involve an incubator facility. An interesting side benefit of the SBIR program is if you have the problem of separating wheat from the chaff in potential tenants for an incubator facility, an award of an SBI grant is kind of like a Good Housekeeping Seal of Approval. You know that one is good.

DR. STEWART: Critical fact I should have mentioned. Remember, you can not win here without being better than a whole lot of other people.

Another fact I did not mention, is the best effort at building a real bridge between small business and the university. Dr. Langerberg is exactly right. In the NSF phase of this, 50 percent of the awards after four years did involve an academic collaboration. The problem is the rest of the government is not doing anywhere near that well.

What I should also have made plain is that when the small businessman gets his first phase award, $50,000, the regs permit him to use up to a third of it with a nonprofit institution or nonprofit faculty member. He can go to a good person on a faculty in his field who is probably better at writing proposals than he is and say, "Look, if you will take a chance on writing a proposal for me, if I win it I will pay you X dollars and you can be my consultant or we can joint venture on some other basis." That's a good way to raise the quality of all proposals.

Second, if he gets a Phase 2 award he may use up to fifty percent of his grant for help from the nonprofit institutions. Now we are talking about dollars in six figures, up to half of a half a million dollars.

On Friday night our institute is going to give out one of its awards to a university which has done, we think, an outstanding job of giving us a pilot model for how this ought to work in one specific case.

DR. YOUNG: Leo Young. I have the responsibility for the SBIR program in DOD, as Milton knows. Ours had a precursor just like NSF, the DSEF program, and then into the full SBIR program back in '83.

Whenever we have a chance to talk about this I always bring up the subject of university-industry cooperation, interaction. Whenever I talk to an audience interested in SBIR I always tell them be sure to involve the university people, don't reinvent the wheel.

And by the same token, when I talk to a university audience, I also mention the SBIR, here is the opportunity for you to get involved in it.

So let me reiterate the same message, and say that it is important to get the important interaction going.

I also happen to have the responsibility for the IR&D program, which has to do with the large companies, and there again I should have said it this morning, I always emphasize the interaction that is possible between big business, if you will, and the universities.

In that case the IR&D program is a little more formalized and we have new guidelines which came out just a few days which spell out how that interaction should take place. The same brochure, although it was held up, did indeed come out just a few days ago and it is full of ideas that were initiated by different components within DOD and the participating agencies are the Navy, Air Force, DARPA and DNA.

One other final comment. Although in Phase 3 normally we would look for private funding, in the case of DOD it is a little bit different since we are involved in production ourselves. We also allow when another DOD component it interested is production on that particular whatever it is development.

73

DR. STEWART: So you will yourselves provide Phase 3?

DR. YOUNG: Exactly.

CHAPTER SIX
"Impacts on Industry: II"

Samuel W. Tinsley
Union Carbide Corporation

Introductory Remarks

Our next speaker, Sam Tinsley, is a graduate of Western Kentucky University. He received his PhD in organic chemistry from Northwestern. He was Assistant Professor of Chemistry at Texas Technological University and then he started with Union Carbide in 1950 as a Research Chemist in South Charleston, West Virginia.

He later became Associate Director for R&D at South Charleston and then in 1972 was named Director of Corporate Research for Union Carbide and in 1978 was appointed Director of Corporate Technology.

More recently he was appointed Director of Technology Planning. He is the holder or coholder of 40 U.S. patents. He is the President of the Industrial Research Institute, past Chairman of the Directors of Industrial Research, and a past President of the Commercial Development Association. Sam is going to talk to us about an especially appropriate topic in 1984, Big Brother Can Help.

SAMUEL W. TINSLEY

For an individual who began in industry many years ago and who obtained patents and published articles in peer-reviewed journals, circumstances under which you are confident that what you are disclosing or saying has not been disclosed or said before, it is extremely frustrating to participate in a forum such as this -- invariably, I find that, whatever points I want to make on almost any subject, someone has said it first and better.

These national Conferences have been blessed with a number of excellent talks on R&D and science policy and its interactions with business. In particular, those of you who were in San Antonio last October and heard Dr. Roland Schmitt of General Electric are current on the subject. Roland provided rationale and development for four guidelines for federal R&D policy. I believe these are worth recalling:

Four Guidelines for Federal R&D Policy

1. Concentrate direct support on academically-based research, not on government-targeted industrial R&D.

2. Concentrate on sunrise science and technology, not on sunrise industries and products.

3. Concentrate on strengthening the climate for privately-based innovation, not on government-selected innovation.

4. Concentrate on development for the government's own needs, not development for market needs.

At this point I should sit down; however, unless I missed it, there is a rather simplistic approach which you may not have seen. First, some assumptions: there is a positive correlation between our investment in R&D and our national security and economic vitality, the enabling function, which constitutes this correlation, is the development of innovative technology.

Finally, an opinion -- the health of the present and foreseeable future balance sheets of the enterprise is the most important determinant of industry's investment in R&D. Thus, while policy initiatives such as tax credits are helpful, they are neither sufficient nor critical.

Now let's define two types of technological innovation:

A. Conservation type -- do what we do but with less materials, energy, capital or labor.

B. New options for society type -- new products, new services, new systems.

With this kind of split, let's look at the organization most likely associated with the two types, particularly, the different impacts of each and the different need priority of each. Then let's consider some factors in resource allocation decisions.

In general, conservation innovations have a low public visibility and a low degree of risk largely dependent upon good old nuts and bolts, first class, process for product engineering; the return can be calculated with a high degree of confidence, usually associated with big companies; of national strategic importance from the standpoint of international competitiveness; major impact is on productivity; highest priority need is capital generation and recovery, to which I will return shortly. This is the area of hope for "rust belt" industries and commodity producers. To illustrate the impact on productivity, I'll use an example from my own company. A few years ago, we receieved our second consecutive Kirkpatrick Award for Chemical Engineering Achievement for our Unipol (R) process for low density polyethylene. This new process required 1/10 the space, 1/5 the energy, and 1/2 the capital than the old process. We are spreading these gains over many millions of pounds of product.

The new options for society types of innovation, on the other hand, have a high public visibility, a high degree of risk, again critically dependent on product and process engineering in addition to marketing and financial management; the rate of return sometimes seems impossible to determine, usually associated with small companies (although some large companies are very proficient), of strategic importance because the major impact is on job creation. This is thought of as the home of "hitech", "biotech", etc.

Let's return to the conservation innovators and would-be innovators and take a look at their highest priority need -- capital, considering both the allocation and size of the capital pool. One reasonable set of allocation priorities might be: first, government mandated expenditures (about 25% in our industry, over 25% in some others), second, extension and expansion of the business (necessary for survival as competitive entity), then straight conservation and new product or new business projects.

Now how about the size of the pool. For a ten year period beginning in 1973, U.S. industry was able to generate a cash flow that was only about 74% of its growth needs. Recall that industry already had a long term debt load that was over 30% of its total invested capital and the problems starts to come into focus -- the tax cut of 1978 and the accelerated depreciation schedules of 1981 were welcomed remedies.

Now a note of concern -- I mentioned polyethylene before -- a product of the petrochemical industry -- an industry fairly well known to Union Carbide since we developed it. A couple of years ago the Department of Commerce did a competitive assessment of the U.S. Petrochemical Industry vis-a-vis the corresponding industry being built up in the Middle East. The critical variable turned out to be a raw material cost factor of 6X to 10X in favor of the Middle East. I'll leave the conclusion to your deduction.

Quite a problem from the standpoint of international competitiveness? Consider a couple more impacts -- the EPA just published a study that estimates that between 1981 and 1990 government and industry will spend $526 billion on air and water pollution controls. The chemical industry's share of this burden was estimated to be $36 billion (10 billion in capital expense and $26 billion for operation and maintenance). Further, the petrochemical segment of this industry is looking down the barrel of a superfund extension bill that would raise costs from today's $300 million per year to about $2 billion per year. You will recall that because of the peculiarities of the superfund legislation, which is designed to raise funds to clean up "orphan" dump sites, the tax is levied on feedstocks and some twelve petrochemical producers wind up paying about 70% of the bill. To put these numbers in some sort of perspective, Business Week reports that, in 1983, the chemical industry spent $3.4 billion on R&D and earned $4 billion.

I make no apologies for departing from the general to specifics -- I believe the government's policies towards, not just clear, but ultra clean, air and water plus its handling of wastes are mandating resource allocations that endanger the egg-laying (R&D) capacity of the goose but the survival of the goose itself.

DR. BAEDER: Don Baeder, Occidental Petroleum. Too often we focus on R&D policies when there are other policies of the government that really are damaging industry's competitiveness, which in turn has to affect R&D. I think there are lot of examples and I appreciate your bringing them up.

DR. TINSLEY: Before most of you consider it and give a big yawn, think about the downstream consequences. These are the building blocks that darn near everything in the business world is made of. Also think about the downstream consequences to chemical and engineering departments when there is no chemical industry.

DR. CHAFFEE: Kim Chaffee from Innotech Corporation. Sam, what is the alternative here with this pollution situation? What would you advocate in this case?

DR. TINSLEY: A reasonable balance. You know the old asymptotic curve, you spend ten percent of the money getting 90 percent out, then you spend 90 percent getting the last ten percent.

I just hope we make sure we really want it and it is really worth what we intend to invest in the next few years.

We are getting to the point where we are fighting the diffusion theory. No, seriously.

I was reading the other day about some deliberations over volative organics in drinking water, I think it was. And they were actually seriously talking about having zero concentrations again. I thought the DeLaney amendment had cured us of trying to assign zero concentrations to anything. Zero changes awfully fast with good analytical research going on. So a reasonable balance. Sure we all want to clean everything. I think it is just a question of how and how much can we afford.

DR. ZAHRT: Ken Zahrt from Dayton. Just occurs to me that this might be another reason for instigating certain industries to leave this nation and move to other countries where such regulations do not exist. Has anybody given any thought to that and used it to help find a solution?

DR. TINSLEY: Well, you have a solution not just to this legislation, but a lot of others. That is a viable solution, move to the place where concentrates, for example, are 50 cents a thousand instead of five dollars a thousand over here, move to the place where the labor rates are considerably lower, move to a

place where you do not have this kind of a burden on your capital
resources.

CHAPTER SEVEN
"Impacts on Industry: III"

Dr. Mary Good
UOP Research Center

Introductory Remarks

DR. LARSON: Our third speaker is Mary Good.   She is a
graduate of Arkansas State Teachers College and has a PhD from
the University of Arkansas. She is currently vice-president and
Director of Research at the Signal-UOP Research Center (the
central laboratory of the Signal Companies, Des Plaines,
Illinois). Previously she has been with the University of New
Orleans and LSU.

Mary is a very active woman. She is President of the Inorganic
Division of the International Union Pure and Applied Chemistry.
She just finished a term as Vice-Chairman of the National Science
Board.   She is a member of the Boards of Directors of the
Industrial Research Institute, of the National Institute for
Petroleum and Energy Research. She is on the Board of Trustees
of RPI. She is a member of the panel for Material Science at the
National Bureau of Standards.   She is on the External Advisory
Committee for the LSU College of Engineering and, very
interestingly, is International Chairman of the Amelia Earhart
Fellowship Committee.

I was pleased to see an article in C&E News that Signal-UOP
had revealed plans for major expansion of its Des Plaines
research center. In the next five years the center is expected
to double its budget and increase its scientific staff more than
seventy percent. And it also noted the center's research budget
for 1984 was up 23 percent from 1983.

Mary   is   going   to   talk   about   the   appropriate
industry-university-government infrastructure.

DR. MARY GOOD

What I wanted to do today was to say something about the whole
business of national science policy. The concept has been around
for a long time. You heard about some of it this morning, so
what I would like to do is talk about the impact of government
policy on industrial laboratories; say a few words about the
impact as it appears with respect to the industry-academic
interface; and try to follow up on some of the questions that
were brought up earlier about small businesses.

81

After listening to Milt I decided it was pointless for us to increase our laboratory support because we fall into that category of companies who apparently have no innovative skills; but Milt, we will do the best we can.

Maybe what he wants me to do is put all of that extra money into small businesses and we do some of that. Half of it he says will do.

But at any rate, it might actually be easier to talk about the impact of national policies on R&D if there were not so many theory paradoxes. No other nation comes even close to spending as much as the United States on R&D, yet perhaps no other nation is presently so vulnerable to being overtaken in the innovation race.

If you look, for example, at the recession we have just gone through, that is the worst recession apparently since the Great Depression. Industry in that period did not cut back on its R&D, it actually spent more than it ever had before and it is continuing to do so. In fact, industry spent so much on R&D that for the first time in memory it surpassed that most generous patron of science -- Uncle Sam.

But everyone is telling industry that is not enough. You must do more! Like it or not, we have indeed been tossed, therefore, into this brier patch to try to figure out what really is a national technology and science policy and how we should interact with it.

For many of us that is not really very comfortable because, trained as we are in the precision of the scientific method, as much as we like to think that the best answers are usually elegantly beautiful in their simplicity, we now find ourselves in the thicket of social policy.

Here the vectors of the problem are usually soft and fuzzy. The answers though often come hard and painfully sharp. No one seems to get out of the thicket without getting poked at least once in his self-interest. And you must forget about the answers being elegant in their simplicity.

If we expect to emerge unscathed from this kind of a thicket we better begin asking and then answering some basic questions in a convincing manner. Like why should there be a national policy on R&D, in whose interests is it to have a strong policy, is it in the interests of our stockholders, is it in the interest of the scientific community, is it in the interest of taxpayers, and is it in the interest of the public?

When I talk about we, permit me to talk more from the narrow viewpoint of the nation's industrial laboratories. Not too long ago, we, the industrial labs, might have taken a back seat at a conference like this one. Government policymakers and university scientists were expected to provide the leadership on these types of questions but the industrial labs have been propelled into a leading place in the nation's R&D network. Recent articles in the Wall Street Journal and the New York Times have spoken of the surging vitality of the industrial laboratories.

And it is quite a turn-around from what it was twenty years ago because today high quality science graduates are turning increasingly to the industrial laboratories because they feel they can realize their potential in that setting.

Industrial scientists are being heard increasingly in places where national policy is being set, such as the Office of Science and Technology Policy, the National Science Foundation, the National Science Board, the White House Science Board and the National Defense Science Board.

Companies that used to be at each other's throats are setting up consortiums to research some of the tougher common problems. At the same time industries are giving more support to the universities and some universities in turn are forging more cooperative and mutually beneficial links with the industry.

In part, the awakening of the slumbering industrial giant, as Frank Press called the phenomena, is the result of a realization by the business community that it better get its R&D efforts into high gear or it will be eating the dust of the Japanese, the Europeans, and even the Soviet bloc.

But it also is partially a result of a national science policy, whether it has been articulated or not and for better or for worse. And it is a policy pursued by the current administration and endorsed by the Congress.

Under that policy the government's direct support of all but basic and defense research has either fallen or remained flat. And the numbers which you saw this morning I believe in some of the charts will bear that out.

The policy is driven by a belief that industry shareholders and not the taxpayers ought to be responsible for doing the research that can generate corporate profits.

The administration believes that it should not subsidize R&D. Rather it believes it should create a private sector climate in which R&D will flourish. I cannot argue with that perception and with that end result.

However, both presidential candidates are expressing the view that a fertile climate should be created by supporting tax credits, easing the antitrust rules and patent law reforms and both candidates say that not only should industry join in, but perhaps even lead the nation's R&D drive.

So here the industrial laboratories are suddenly thrust into a dominant role, seemingly before we have even had a chance to ask what are we doing here anyway.

As we all know, the relationship between the industrial labs, the universities and the national laboratories, is a delicate and mutually supportive one. If anything, the recent emergence of industrial labs as one of the equal partners is long overdue, but arguing over which of the three should be in the dominant role is a pointless debate.

What we do know is that national science policy should give reign to, for lack of better terminology, scientific democracy. It is based on the same notion that drives our form of government and our economy, that the public interest somehow, and perhaps miraculously, emerges even from the chaotic stew of conflicting interests, opinions and constituencies.

Any national science policy, to be successful, must also recognize the same kind of diversity in the scientific and technological community. That the risky, the apparently off-beat and the independent-minded need to be cultivated. That innovation blossoms in the most unexpected corners. That science and technology advance by serendipity and by chance in the most frustratingly unplanned ways.

And I must say there are times when I worry a bit about some of the papers which are being published in the academic community today, where they are attempting to analyze why industrial research actually produces good things and they are making a major effort to put numbers, quanititative numbers, on research productivity.

My feeling is that may not only be a task which is going to be very difficult to do, but if successful or worse, perceived to be successful, it may even be quite dangerous because it will put in place a method, if you will, of how things are funded and how CEO's who are not technically trained choose to make a choice between research projects.

My judgment is that will get us into very big trouble very quickly and if the big laboratories and big companies choose to go that way, Milton is correct at that point. The only hope you have is for a very arbitrary small business owner to make his own

84

way.

That means that national policy must leave the door open for innovation at as many as labs as possible, whether they be university, national or industrial.

But why should national policy be concerned at all about the industrial laboratories? Doesn't private enterprise, economic democracy, does not that assume that risk goes right along with making a profit? That if five years of research goes down the tubes those are the breaks of a free market economy? And that the public and the taxpayers should not be made to pay for the risk because they do not get to share in the profits?

Generally I agree with the argument that it is the shareholders and management who should take the risk.

But the formulators of national science policy and the public need to ask whether the kinds of research needed for a healthy economy and healthy society will get done by leaving the industrial labs entirely in a void.

They need to recognize that some pure research simply is not profitable and this is the kind of research that is first needed to commercialize a product or a technology. They need to recognize that it is difficult to turn some kinds of research into a marketable product or technology. That the research can produce a technology that may be obsolete just a year after introduction. That industrial research often is alley with dark corners and dead ends.

They need to recognize that some of this research, even though potentially beneficial for society, will go undone because it is too risky for business, does not interest the universities and is actually unfunded by the government.

A prime example is research into commercially viable ways to deal with the nation's environmental questions, such as water quality and air pollution.

And I have some sympathy with Sam's remarks and particularly since it is so difficult to get the kind of research done that will help with the costs of some of these types of activities.

Nor can private enterprise, left on its own, be expected to pick up the tab for meeting the nation's strategic needs.

When private enterprise decides whether to tackle research on things of strategic national importance, such as alternate sources of energy, it must ask itself which is greater, the potential for profit far down the road or the risk of throwing money, this year and the next year and the next, into what ultimately may be a futile effort.

I do not think I need to explain how the chief executive and head of a lab who is under pressure to minimize expenses might respond to that kind of question.

National science policy makers also need to recognize, in the words of Roland Schmitt, who heads General Electric's corporate research and development, "In a free enterprise system governments not only do not create the markets for products, but are notoriously slow in reacting to shifts in the market place. They lack the crucial entrepreneurial spirit to perceive or acknowledge opportunities early in their development."

National science policy then should encourage, but not direct. It should provide incentives, but not penalize. It should inspire and not dampen with the soggy weight of bureaucratic regulations.

There have been many proposals to accomplish this, such as patent law reform and the removal of some antitrust prohibitions that make scientific cooperation between interested parties difficult, if not impossible.

But today I would like to talk about one in particular, and this is the R&D tax credit. And Sam made the comment that this is a nice thing to have, but not necessarily an essential.

I am going to take that on from the following point of view. The R&D tax credit, in my view, is one of those issues which in a sense is a "bell weather." If it is not exteneded it will say to the industry and to CEO's that the government and the country do not believe that research is important.

So whether or not you work out a theory which says that in reality the tax credit is not important is not the key point. From a sociological impact, I think it is crucial.

It was established as you know, by the Economic Recovery Act of 1981 as part of an effort to get this nation moving out of the recession. You get a 25 percent tax credit for new spending on R&D above and beyond the average annual amount you spent during the three prior years. The first year for claiming credits was in 1983. The credit has been a major factor, in my opinion, in pushing industrial R&D to record levels.

Now, there are all kinds of questions about that. There are all kinds of arguments that some people cheat and have put things in that they would not have otherwise, and I suspect all of those things are true.

But, you know, we have lots of laws in the United States which have the potential for being misused, but that does not mean that we should throw them out simply because somebody misuses them along the way.

The credit, I believe, has been a major factor in maintaining funding levels for R&D. It expires at the end of 1985 and I think that is a pity for the nation and for the industry unless it can be extended.

Not only should the credits be made permanent, but they should really be fine-tuned to provide even more incentives more effectively.

If you want to know whether the credits were an effective incentive, you should ask the people who use them. An Ad Hoc Electronics Tax Group representing the top twenty companies in the field, including the Signal Companies, said they are.

Arguing for making the credits permanent, the group said that American's high-tech companies already pay too large a share of the taxes. They cited studies that show the corporate tax rate for high-tech firms runs between 22 percent and 27 percent, compared with an overall corporate rate of about 16 percent.

If high-tech companies are expected to lead us into the bright sunshine of the new economy, they at least should not be paying more than their fair share of taxes for the privilege, particularly since if you look at their risk factor it normally is quite high.

Well, some might argue, industry was going to increase its R&D expenditures anyway, even without the credits. And obviously it is true you cannot prove a direct cause and effect correlation between the fact that industrial R&D investments reached an all-time high just as the tax credits went into effect.

But it sure is an interesting coincidence. And I can tell you as the director of research for the 54th largest industrial company in the nation, that some things just would not and will not get done without the margin provided by the credit.

It is the credit, for example, in my laboratory that provides the extra incentive to take a technology developed in the university and the national laboratory and massage it into a commercially viable product or process. In many ways it is the edge, if you will, it is the fringe area where you can afford to spend some money on highly chancy things. And one of the ways that you get technology transfer from the university, that is really very risky if I go out there and look at all of the universities and all of the ideas there are, but if I have a little money at the fringes, and particularly if I get a little extra tax credit for it, well, all right, we will give it a try and see what we can do with that. And that is how some of these things get done.

For example, in our own laboratory at the moment we have a major interest in industrial enzymology. And as many of you might know, there is a major effort in the universities today in the whole area of artificial enzymes. There is no way, without the extra that the tax credit gives, that I could get my CEO to put money in anything as far down the road as artificial enzymes, but with that little bit he is willing to do that, to span the bridge between industrial enzymology. Real new chemistry all of a sudden becomes a possibility and a reality.

It is just that little extra encouragement that is needed normally to keep a project alive through the many twists and turns and temporary reversals on the way to successful commercialization.

Making the tax credit permanent would give industrial laboratories the stability they need in order to make rationale plans for future R&D expenditures.

Most R&D projects are long term, five years or more, with the greatest expenditures coming at the end of the period. So the current three year window is not as effective as a permanent credit. And one of the problems why industry has not responded as well as it might is a CEO's seeing the end of that in three years.He or she might say oh, my goodness, if I get myself into that bind and I have this tax credit, then I am stuck all of a sudden with money I have spent. I am going to have to cut back and I do not want to do that.

Without the certainty of a permanent credit, too, some companies no doubt are tempted to hold off on increasing their expenditures on deserving projects so they do not increase their base on which the credit is figured in later years. Those of you who have good controllers understand that very well. Spending that extra money now would only reduce the amount of their credit later on. There are other problems with the current law that need to be addressed.

For a credit to be an incentive, a company first must be profitable. And I think this one addresses some of Milt's concerns as well. An approach needs to be worked out that will encourage companies that are in the red to undertake needed R&D, which eventually could put them back in the black.

Companies just starting off do not get credit either. They

need the incentives as well. Also advisable would be changes that exclude a company from getting credit for duplicating another company's product. We do a lot of that in American industry and Milt is correct in the sense that this practice does not help us much in competition overseas or very many other places.

Companies also should not get credits for research that adapts an existing product that meets the needs of a particular customer or for developing new or improved characteristics that relate to style and consumer taste, rather than to consumption.

All of these things might qualify for credits under the existing law and we really ought to be looking for the kind of research that makes a meaningful difference.

There also should be an expansion of the credit for companies that contract with universities to perform basic research and that contribute certain scientific equipment to those schools. Many of these provisions, including the permanent extension of the credits, were included in legislation that had bipartisan sponsorship and the backing of both Reagan and Mondale.

With that kind of support, you might ask, how can it fail? Well, it did in the first round. It was killed for this session during a recent House-Senate conference on taxes. Congressman Dan Rostenkowski, a Democrat who calls home not far from our Signal UOP Research Center, and Chairman of the House Ways and Means Committee, indicated that he opposed the legislation because it would further trim tax revenues during trying budgetary times.

Some people estimate that the three-year package will eventually cost about two billion in lost revenue, but no one can be sure. But like the Japanese and others whom we so admire for their leap ahead in the technological race, we have to ask ourselves what are the long-term payoffs? Clearly we are dealing with issues that require an investment, which as Webster says, is a commitment of money for future return.

Industry has been highly criticized in the past, and correctly so, for being short-sighted, for having an eye too close to the balance sheet and the stock market tables. Here is a policy that will encourage long-term thinking on the part of American industry. And it is a policy that really should get everyone's support.

So what's to worry? The betting in Washington is that the tax credit extension legislation will reappear after the election and ultimately be passed.

Well, everyone now is talking about how they are friends of

high-tech, and that is the vogue. And I liked Milt's analogy this morning about the five to 12, but we know how styles change and indeed how rapidly they can change and we also know how friends disappear after elections.

Might I suggest to this conference that we remind our friends in Washington that this is a particular type of promise we would expect them to keep.

I would like to finish by saying a couple of things about the whole university-industry interface and what that means. The basic research base in the United States has been praised by almost everybody and it is true that it is probably the best in the world. It is also true that we have not been making as good use of the base, our own base, as our competitors have managed to do. The question is what do we do about that?

My feeling is that the best of the university-industry relationships are those that involve people. We wrote a report for the National Science Foundation on the university-industry relationship and it turns out that those relationships that had actual products, if you will, over time and were really very satisfactory, were those in which you had direct interaction between individuals.

This is another area where having a governmental organization does not help you very much. In fact it can get in the way. What you want is people to talk to people. That is beginning to happen.

Industry is beginning to understand that it needs to move things from the basic research area as rapidly as it possibly can to products and processes. And left to their own doing, I think the universities and industry will work out most of the problems. There will be lots of friction. There will be lots of discussion, but I think it is a workable solution.

The government can help in a sense by again providing incentives, but hopefully not putting together infrastructure so you have energy barriers that have to be climbed every time you want to have an appropriate interaction with the university or vice versa.

So I think that conferences of this kind, where people from all three segments sit down and talk to each other are a lot more valuable, regardless of whether the speakers say anything signficiant really, but the fact that you can sit down and talk to each other and visit at the coffee breaks and visit over dinner is probably the most important issue of the entire conference.

DISCUSSION

DR. ZAHRT: Ken Zahrt again. I recall a few years back -- I do not think it was last year -- but one of the points brought out was the time factor in achieving successful products from research and with the government regulatory changes industry had a very short time perspective in these matters, three to five years.

I have not heard this addressed from any of the speakers and I wonder if that still exists or if the environment is changing with respect to industry's perspective?

I know 40 years ago five years was a long time for industry and it still appeared to be that way a few years ago. Can any of you address yourself to the time factor and its relationship to all that has been discussed here?

DR. GOOD: I will make a couple of comments and then let somebody who has been in the business longer give you some better perspective. It is very hard to get data but it is my perception that if you go through the industrial laboratories today, there are things that are very different from what was true twenty years ago -- let's go back right after the war. There were some excellent industrial laboratories then that were built in the late fifties and early sixties. The best description I can give you for them is they were show pieces and served the PR purposes for the companies.

They did outstanding fundamental research, but they were simply duplicates, for all practical purposes, of the universities, except that they were high quality research institutes.

Those laboratories died for the most part simply because when times got tough people did not understand why those were necessary things to support. That has changed and if you go into industrial laboratories today, one of the things you will find is that most of them have state of the art equipment and state of the art people. We can attract today the very best brains that the university turns out and that is a change because that was not true 25 years ago. And in that sense, industry is making a commitment to the longer term in that it will build the technology if that is the only way it can get it.

You cannot have every project, however, in your laboratory designed to come to fruition in 1990. There has to be spill-out along the way.

What most people are doing is trying to build some basic

91

strengths in technologies with the hope they can have some spin-off when profit kinds of things come out in the early years, and really major contributions come five years down the line. And I think a lot of that kind of strategic planning is going on.

DR. TINSLEY: I think the crack about industry being relatively short-termed and short-sighted is like most generalities, sort of a bad rap.

I mentioned that polyethylene process we announced in 1977. We started the first work on that in 1959.

One of our responses to the again sort of conservation type-survival type research, the OPEC reality in 1973. I do not know whether any of you remember how soon we were going to project $100 a barrel oil.

One of our responses was to lay the laboratory basis at least for processes that will convert coal or synthesis gas or methanol to the entire spectrum of organic chemical products. And at that time we were talking in the nineties. Right now it looks like we may be talking about the two-thousands.

But there is a fairly healthy balance, I think, between fairly long-term, fairly short-term and intermediate-term R&D. It varies all over the lot. It depends on the company, your position in your national competitive market, and your position on the international competitive market.

DR. SPATES: Jim Spates of the Department of the Army. Those of us who are concerned with federal laboratories find ourselves beseiged by one group or another looking for duplicative research. That implied, I think, unnecessarily duplicative research, of course. Whether it is made of inhouse people or independent people or groups, very little is found at least within the Department of Defense historically.

On the other hand, when those of us in the Department of Defense take IR&D review trips we see large amount of duplicative research. Again whether it is necessary or unnecessary is a value judgment.

I would suggest within the private sector commercialization domain, as Mary Good said, there is a lot of duplicative activity. I prefer to call some of it coattail research. It is not real research.

And I pose to Mary Good and the panel the question what might be done about that so they can answer the issue that was brought up earlier today, how do we improve the effectiveness of R&D?

DR. GOOD: That is an enormously difficult question and there is indeed a great deal of coattail type research that goes on in what they believe is other industry technology. It is not just coattail on the government's and whatever.

You know, there is a very fine line between coattail research and technology transfer in the sense of going from government laboratory research to a commercial product.

I have had a lot of experience with particularly some of the national laboratories that are run by the Department of Energy. One of the problems you have is that the people that work in those laboratories come up with what they believe are really very viable ideas, and in many cases they are, but what they do not have any feeling for is what it means to take that idea from a bench scale proof of principle to a product or a process in the market place.

And much of what appears to be coattail research, if it is done correctly, is just that. It is the transfer of a proof of principle kind of thing that comes out of government laboratory into a commercial product.

There is a very fine line between those two. What you hope is that you have research directors and companies that really understand the difference. I surely won't say that they all do, but you have to realize that what looks in many cases like duplicative research is simply a proof that what was written in a paper or done at government laboratory can be repeated, number one. And secondly, can it then be extended into a commercial product.

It is very costly and takes a very long time. One of the things we would like to see is people doing some collaborative things at that point, but that is hard to do. The legalities of doing that get in the way and I think Sam could elaborate on that.

DR. TINSLEY: Well, not really. We are basically a competitive society. One of the reasons we enjoy pretty low prices relative to the rest of the world in a lot of cases in terms of the number of hours we have to work to buy a given thing is that we have a very competitive market place. And as long as we have a competitive market place, you are going to see a certain amount of duplicate research going on in laboratories, certainly in industry and you have to. And I do not know any way out of that one.

DR. GOOD: There is one issue that does concern me today. Some basic research going on in the universities and in some of the national laboratories has already been done very well and in very

93

productive ways, in industrial laboratories but because of proprietary considerations cannot be discussed. I do not know what to do about that.

DR. KRUYTBOSCH: I am Carlos Kruytbosch, with the National Science Foundation. My question really follows on, I guess, the notion of duplicate research.

I worked on the National Science Board-National Science Foundation studies of industry-university relationships. One of the rather startling developments, I thought, was the emergence of the modes of cooperative research, where multiple companies were working with universities and even in the electronics industry, semiconductor industry, working to develop industry cooperative modes to do common research. And this is kind of fascinating because one has had the stereotype of industries jealously guarding their research from each other and so forth.

I think there is still a lot of questions that remain as to how the balance is kept between what they share and they keep to themselves. I wonder whether you have any observations on their trend? I do not think anybody has really mentioned or talked about this trend yet.

DR. GOOD: I think what you asked is "what are we getting for these collaborative kinds of things, is there anything that comes out of them today or where are we with them?"

DR. KRUYTBOSCH: Where are we with them?

DR. GOOD: Where are we with them at the moment? It turns out that in many of these collaborative things, the best examples are still in the incubator stage and I think the count is still out. The microelectronics effort, for example, down at the University of Texas, which has such a large group of the electronics companies involved. I think that is an excellent test case to see whether this kind of thing will work.

I am familiar with that one because we just looked at whether or not we wanted to buy in. The price is very high, and if you do not have a specific interest, you are probably not going to participate. So it is going to be interesting to see how they come out.

Now, some of the collaborative kind of things going on in the university are pretty productive, where companies are getting together, three or four of them, and making grants to a university, with motives directed toward a technology, or the beginnings of a technology, which they can share in.

DR. MILBERG: Egils Milberg, Department of Commerce. I want

94

to ask Mary Good and Milton Stewart a question about the R&D tax credit.

Mary, I think you made a number of good observations about the elusiveness of the R&D tax credits.

For example, you pointed out as you try to and if indeed reduce R&D spending that reduces your future tax benefits. If indeed you are going to reduce R&D spending, there is incentive to drive R&D down even further to establish a low base to capture the benefit of future tax benefits.

You mentioned the companies that do not increase R&D spending do not get any credit, at all so if you are spending a billion dollars you cannot take advantages. You mentioned small business start-up that is not profitable cannot take advantage of the credit either.

Instead of making a permanent extension maybe you put a new formula for incentive for R&D. Let me ask what your response to the following proposal might be. Instead of the 25 percent incremental feature on a rolling base, suppose we had a credit provided for on the base of R&D spending of say like ten percent like an investment tax credit. As you know, investment tax credit goes to plant equipment. R&D tends to be labor intensive, and so on.

And so we put those on par, if you will, and for the case of companies who aren't profitable and this is where I would like Milt to respond, is an investor who puts money into R&D, be it an R&D limited partnership or company who decides to invest, they are capable of taking a tax credit against income, a profitable situation.

So I am wondering with all the problems with the incremental R&D tax credit what appears to be not a very clear correlation between that incremental tax credit and R&D performance in industry, whether or not indeed we might not be considering some other alternative way to calculate such credit?

DR. GOOD: I have no problems with considering other alternatives. The only comment I would make is there is no such thing as a perfect piece of legislation in this field. Because industry is so diversified, I do not think it is possible to put together one piece of legislation which is going to address all the issues we talked about. And if you put in a flat rate you will get some problems, they will just be stated differently. You know what I am saying. There will be other problems associated with that.

My feeling is never mind those problems. And they are severe and certainly should be looked at. On the other hand, my feeling is that you simply have to weigh the risk/benefit ratio, if you will, and I think you have to look at the risk versus the benefit. It will take five years to redo it, in my opinion, with the pace of the current legislative proceeding.

My feeling is we can go with a three-year extension, if you like, and worry about it in the interim because the real problem is going to be if we end up with a discontinuity.

DR. TINSLEY: Egils, I would like to briefly comment. We mentioned the uncertainty a factor while ago and the fact, it did have an end. And it is very difficult to describe what uncertainty does to business management. That is really difficult. We think we know how to handle risk, right, and we spend a lot of time trying to manage risk, but uncertainty puts the whole thing on tilt.

If you are a golfer, this is the closest example I can use. It means somebody stood up behind you as you were ready to hit the ball and said shank.

One other example comes from a model up north of us. It is my understanding Canada has gone to a system where if you can not use that tax credit you can sell it. I think that would take care of the refunding question for the small start-up company that is still unprofitable. You might ask how that is working out.

DR. STEWART: I could not be more pleased that Mary brought up the R&D credit. Many of her comments I agree with entirely.

If I can, let me just mention that I think there is a real risk it will not be extended, despite all the things we have all been told.

It seems to me the two things we have to come to grips with or perhaps three, one of them has been mentioned and that is the fact that serious scholars like Ed Mansfield, will get up and say I cannot find any evidence that it made any difference.

Now, I respectfully submit, number one, he is asking the wrong question and, number two, he is asking it five years too soon.

However, in the first year of the credit, according to Buck Chapman's testimony, the credit cost the revenue 800 million dollars. And I do not care who the president is, that is going to be a stopper. And when he is then told, as Buck testified, that half the benefit went to fewer than 60 companies, then he is going to say we are giving it away. I cannot keep on doing it.

Now, that is really what I think we have to come to grips with and I honestly think we must come up with anything much better than what we have -- we have to come up at least with a cut and paste job that meets enough of the criticism that is going to be made so we can ride it through without any interruption.

Now, here our problem is the private sector is not very good at getting its act together, in case you haven't noticed, when it is confronted by this kind of a problem.

Let me give you an example. I have never told this in public before. This has to do with the SBIR program. When that program was first discussed most seriously after the five years of NSF experiment, I was Chief Counsel for Advocacy at the SBA. And I saw two issues coming along that were going to pit small business and universities against one another in the Congress, and that was one of them.

I called the man I was told was the principal lobbyist in Washington for the major research universities in this country and I said to him, "We are going to have two very bad hair-pullings that are going to be very bad for the community you represent and the one that I am sort of working for. I think it would be a great thing if we got five people from your crowd and five from mine to sit down right now, a year or two before this gets to blood on the floor."

He called me back a few days later and said he had checked around and there was no point to it. End of story, except they wound up spending a million and a half dollars they could have used very well some other way trying to beat the bill we were talking about and we wound up spending the equivalent in energy, because we do not have the cash and wound up with five roll call votes on the floor of the House of Representatives after six months of bitter battle, which nobody needed.

Now, I tell you that because I think that reflects a problem about the making of national science policy we have not licked.

The government can call all the meetings it wants to about all the alleged principles in the science and technology field, but the government does not always, A, know who they are or, B, act like it.

We have to find some way in the private sector to take care of our own business and to get together in time to get these things worked out. And I have to tell you, small business is the worst offender because it is never aware of what is happening until five minutes too late and runs up there screaming you cannot do this to it, or do not pass the bill or whatever.

97

Again if there is one thing I think most tax specialists would agree about our code, apart from its complexity, is that it discourages risk. This is the fatal flaw in our present business tax system, in our present personal tax system. The R&D credit was a very welcome open window. We dare not lose it. I think we are going to unless we find a way to meet some of the criticisms that have been made.

DR. LARSON: Sam, you said that the R&D tax credit was nice to have, but not critical, and Mary mentioned it is important symbolically to make this R&D tax credit permanent. Would you agree that it is important symbolically to make it permanent?

DR. TINSLEY: Sure. I was talking about the life or possible death of an industry and compared to that credits are really not critical. No, it is very nice and as far as redoing the whole thing, we have already been through all the agonies of the lawyers and accountants defining what is qualified, what is not qualified. We even have two sets of books so we can display to business managers that even though that does not show on the R&D line in their operating and revenue segment, because taxes come in way down here after operating income, it really means they have credit on their R&D line up here.

DR. RISEN: I am Bill Risen from Brown University. I wanted to take the chance to continue a line that Mary Good started earlier having to do with university-industry cooperation and research and bring up one problem with it, one essentially practical, logistical problem, because I think there are some ideas to kick around that probably would help all of us think about that.

That is, if you estimate there are, say, a couple of hundred industrial concerns that would be interested in this and a couple hundred research universities that would be interested in it, there is something like ten to the fifth possible one by one interactions. And the ways of finding the one out of the ten to the fifth that are proper for you and the ways of finding those individuals in universities who have the potential for contributing very productively but who are not the stars you like to identify as the expert in the field you are interested in this year, but could indeed be very useful as collaborators.

It is an enormously difficult logistical problem and from everybody from organizations like Council for Chemical Research, the American Chemical Society, in the chemistry area and the equivalent ones in a number of other professional fields are trying very hard to find ways to do it. And perhaps if not only you, Mary, but others on the panel and others joining in the conference have some practical suggestions as to how to make those marriages, that would be very helpful.

DR. GOOD: Bill that is an age old problem. The difficulty you get into if you put together organizational structure that has no real reason for being, people will not respond. It is really that straightforward. The difficulty is you would like for as many as people to get involved as you can. I think the universities in a sense are a little bit naive frankly in this area. Having been in both segments, I can say that without getting stoned, hopefully, but I do think they are naive in the sens of what the industry can afford to pay for in terms of university interaction.

The point is that the industry has never had a problem finding appropriate academic consultants. That has been going on since time immemorial. If you look at that study the NSF did, you find the real long-lasting interactions, almost 80 percent of them started that way because they got the fellow involved and he came to the company, figured out what was going on, he had another colleague who knew something about something else and the whole thing just grows.

The real problem is, a lot of my academic colleagues simply sit in the university community assuming that the industrial laboratories and what they were doing is the same as it was twenty years ago when they were a student. They have had no interaction with it since and have made no effort to find out what goes on there. They simply believe it looks the same as it used to, so they do not have much of an interest.

They have the feeling that somebody from the industry ought to come and pat them on the shoulder and say, "I need you." That is just not going to occur. People are going to have to get out there and stir around a little bit and they are going to have to put some time -- and that I find my academic colleagues extremely reluctant to do -- they are going to have to put a little bit of their time into some of these interactive kinds of things.

They are going to have to be willing to sit on some panels, be willing to get involved in some joint efforts. There are hundreds of them today where there is real possibility for interactive discussions between industry and the academic group.

The people from the academic community that I have heard the most complaints from are those who absolutely will not, even when asked, sit on those kinds of interactive kinds of things.

Industry is not without its blame either because some of the ones in industry do the same. They do not believe there is anything of interest to them out there.

So all you can do is build it little by little and the CCR and the Council for Chemical Research is certainly a way to begin. I think that CCR has certainly been very productive in introducing people to what is going on.

If I look around, nearly all of the academicians here today I personally know one way or the other. The problem is that they are the same ones I have seen in these kinds of interactive meetings before.

DR. FUNDINGSLAND: Osmund Fundingsland, US General Accounting Office. With respect to the R&D set aside for small business, as most of you probably know, that program has a finite life with a sunset clause and it has several objectives.

Obviously the things that have been referenced here already provide some measures of the impact of the program, namely those that deal with the follow-on funding.

Those companies that go through Phases 1 and 2 successfully and then get additional government funding outside of the set aside program, and those companies which win private sector funding for continuation of the technology they have generated or developed initially under the set aside program, will be considered to have shown some degree of success.

There are two other objectives in the legislation, however, that are very difficult to measure. One is the degree to which this set aside program for R&D for small business and nonprofits has enhanced innovation, technological innovation and how it has enhanced commercialization. Now, the GAO has done some studies in the past of reviewing other work that has been done on assessing innovation and the popular claim to small business contributes a greater share than is generally acknowledged in the innovation process, and depends how you define innovation also. In exploring previous work, we have found there is no consensus really on what kind of definition you need, what kind of indicators are good measures and how you really assess the impact of small business innovation and commercialization, or for that matter, the degree of innovation generated by any business in a very quantitative way.

The question I have for the panel, any of you, is what do you know about what is being done by the executive branch or other groups like the institute you mentioned earlier, to identify what needs to be done in way of data generation or conception indicators or measures that can be used before the program has reached its sunset phase to clearly show in a quantitative way or some quantitative way the degree to which it has succeeded in enhancing the innovation process and the commercialization by small business?

100

DR. STEWART: The question asked is almost the kind of ultimate science research question I gave up trying to answer a long time ago. The debatability of practically everything anybody says about this is, I am afraid, not to be ended entirely by data.

In this particular field, especially by the time you get through listening to any two economists, I think you feel desperate about how you would ever satisfy anyone. I have to introduce it that way. We are trying. That is all I can tell you. I mean if we had enough money, yes, we could help you.

Let me tell you what we are trying to do. We sent out a questionnaire to the first 360 winners of SBIR grants in the period that Dr. Langenberg was talking about (those who won since the passage of the act have not had time to show results). We have 160 responses. That was a great disappointment to me. We had to work very hard to get 160 of them.

We knew they would not tell the government anything and we didn't think they would tell us either. So we said we will get Price Waterhouse in between us and them and we will make them swear on a Bible they will never tell what happened to any one company. That system was set up. The 160 returns are being coded now.

The difficulty begins when you start talking about technology impact. Once you get past the grossest level, that "A company licensed B company to take technology that was developed in the SBIR Program" and you get to things like "The SBIR work we did got us interested in something else. We started out in a photography-related field and we wound up, of all things, in photosynthesis in some biological application. Some other company is now tramping into the future with the result of what we did."

I do not mean to be despairing about this, although short of somebody coming up with a couple of million dollars, I do not think, in the time frame we have, we can answer this question definitively. All we do is answer it anecdotally.

Let me give you an example of an evaluator's ultimate answer. Whatever the apparent direct results, they are going to say "that is well and good, but how about the people who did not get SBIR awards? How do you know it made any difference? How do you know they did not go out and raise even more money? How do you know you did not get in the way of the free market funding of R&D projects, these people in Washington cooking up these R&D subjects did not actually divest from research some more important areas?"

101

That is what I call the "fruitless-endless evaluator process" and the federal government is better at it than anybody I know.

What I think you are reduced to is common sense. You have to look at the process, look at what happened to the companies that did or did not win in a gross way and anecdotally say this happened often enough or it did not happen often enough to make us think this is worth doing or not worth doing.

The five-year sunset was dubious from the beginning. It's just not enough time, for a full demonstration study.

Why did we ask for Phase 3? Private sector people fought for it. We do not want government people trying to outguess the market place. We wanted them to have market judgments from someone before they put out large dollars.

DR. LASKER: My name is Lorraine Lasker from New York Medical College. I have a comment and then a question to Mr. Stewart.

First the comment. In your talk you mentioned the state of New York had its matching support for the SBIR Program. I just wanted to bring to your attention and to others here, I do not know how many other states have these programs, but the New York State, through its Science and Technology Foundation, has a program of grants to universities who reach out to businesses in the state for manufacturing and distribution of products, potential products, that you may have ready for patents or just had patented.

We did participate in the competition and we are the first health science institution in New York State to receive an award under the program.

There is a second program about which I have just seen an RFP. It is grants to small businesses in the state who wish to improve their manufacturing processes through research and need to reach out perhaps for consulting or other support to universities. So the notice goes to both groups. And I think this is the first round under that program. I just thought you may be interested in looking at some of these other programs because they certainly lend themselves to federal extension. It is a modest program in the state of New York. That is the comment.

Now the question, also having to do with the relation of small business to what Don Langenberg brought up about research parks. I wondered, Mr. Stewart, if you have any information about the effect of research parks on the small business or on the universities? Since the business by its nature is entrepreneurial and semi-proprietary, I wondered what the effect might be. Research parks are growing up all over and we particularly are involved in the development of a biomedical medical research park in Westchester County.

DR. STEWART: On your comment, first, our major project as an institute for next year -- I should have mentioned we want the help of anybody we can get -- to organize up to 100 small business-university technology councils, very modest things, with five or ten faculty people and five or ten small business people from parallel disciplines who know one another, to sit down and review SBIR proposals in pairs, just to pick people in their states who are competent from both communities to work together to prepare proposals. We think that will do what happened in NSF.

As Dr. Langenberg mentioned, half of their proposals wound up being collaborations between universities and small businesses. If we can bring that off we think that will happen even more.

Second, on industrial parks, I have to crayfish my answer this way. Number one, if I were a college president I would want one around the corner absolutely.

I think Stanford's brilliance, Dean Terman's brilliance when he established their industrial park these many years ago, has been confirmed again and again in enough places.

It is a fact that entrepreneurs really do not care much for the rest of the human race. They only like other entrepeneurs. If you can get five of them into an industrial park, it will attract others. They love to steal ideas, people, all sorts of things from one another. They love to swap war stories. And so the industrial park, I think, makes great sense in terms of what I know about entrepreneurs. And that is what everybody ought to be concerned with. That is point one.

Point two, I think you must be terribly patient now because this is becoming the fad of the generation. Everybody is building one. I honestly do not know how many the society can support.

If I can tie a few things together, one of the things I hope to negotiate with Mary and others is, for example, the R&D credit I think maybe ought to go in an incremental way to a big company which gives work to a small company to encourage big companies to spin out some R&D. She wants to hire the people herself.

Phase 3 commitment ought to be eligible for R&D credit. In the same way, when you deal with R&D park matters I am not enough of real estate person to know what determines whether they are successful or not, but I have to tell you an awful lot of them are going to fail, in my opinion.

They are going to fail as matters of real estate investment, not because there shouldn't be R&D parks. It is because they are going to be in the wrong place or a porr job is going to be done of selecting the kinds of companies that go into them. No bridges, no good enough bridges, are built between the university and the companies, between large companies and small ones. Just having an R&D park's shingle out there is not going to have sense behind it. That is about as much nonwisdom as I have.

DR. GOOD: With respect to helping with your people problem, Bill, one of the things we could do, there are a number of vice-presidents for research from the universities in the audience and we could make a rule that any meeting which has university, industrial and government people to which those vice-presidents for research are invited, they cannot come unless they bring one faculty member with them and they can not bring the same one twice.

CHAPTER EIGHT
"Impacts on the Government: I"

Albert Teich
American Association For The
Advancement of Science

Introductory Remarks

MR. HAHN: In the next ninety minutes we are going to have, I think, an interesting session looking at the impacts on government of the Reagan Administration's science and technology policy, actions and pronouncements. We each have our own images, not only from what Jim Ling gave us yesterday, but from the President, the Director of the Office of Management and Budget, Science magazine and from what many other sources have told us about this particular idea or activity. This administration's approach has a different flavor from the last, as did the one before it.

We have asked two very outstanding practitioners -- observers of science and technology policy -- to lead our discussion. In particular, we picked two people who are known for their articulateness and their objectiveity. They also have two additional very critical characteristics: one is they have been observing this scene very, very closely from different perspectives, and, two, they are not part of the Administration. So I invite you to listen and to compare what they are saying.

They are going to touch a bit on the history of the last four years. Compare what they say to Jim Ling's version yesterday. Deviations will be significant but I think it will be equally significant where these views coincide.

This is not be a hatchet or other type of negative operation whatsoever. We will attempt to get alternative views of what S&T policy looks like from those who are not responsible for pursuing it. Our first speaker is Al Teich. The general subject Al will talk about is the evolution of the Reagan science and technology policy.

Chris Hill, from the Congressional Research Service, will look at major trends and present some personal ideas and observations because Chris has had the big advantage of being both on the inside and the outside. He is now another type of insider working on Capitol Hill.

Our format will be for Al to talk to us for approximately 25 minutes and we will discuss his ideas. Then Chris in the same format. I will add a few remarks from still a different viewpoint now that I am called a Futurist. Several of you have been unkind enough to say, "Whatever happened to Walter, where did he go wrong?" Well, you will get to make a judgment on that later.

Al Teich is now, we are happy to say, the Head of Public Sector Programs at the Office of the Advancement of Science. He is no newcomer to that particular organization or job, but now he is in charge of the Section and that probably makes a big difference. He has been with the AAAS since 1980. He was a professor at George Washington University.

Before that he was at the State University of New York as Director of Research on Public Policy Alternatives. He was originally trained as a physicist and has a degree in political science from MIT. Al, it's all yours.

DR. ALBERT TEICH

There have been many changes in federal R&D policy over the past several years. I would like to review some of those changes and put them into an analytical framework that might help in understanding them.

My general approach centers on the notion that science and technology policies are not made in a vacuum. They are shaped by broader political and social currents in our society. The science policy community -- that is, the group of organizations, institutions and individuals who devote their efforts mainly to influencing science and technology policy directly -- has relatively little control over these currents. What this community has done over the past several years, however, has been to act as a moderating influence, damping out the more radical changes and helping to maintain equilibrium in the system.

What are these broader currents? I see three principal ones as having influenced the shape of science and technology policy over the past several years.

The first is the changing set of perceptions and attitudes towards national defense. The second is our national and international economic situation, changing understanding of that situation, and changing thoughts about how to deal with it. And, third, is the complex set of changing perceptions and attitudes towards the role of government in society. That is a very important current, one which was heavily influenced, of course, by the outcome of the 1980 presidential election.

To see how these factors have influenced science and technology policy in recent years, let us review the evolution of

106

the current administration's science policy, beginning with the period just prior to the 1980 election, when the nation was choosing between Ronald Reagan and Jimmy Carter. Science and technology did not play a very large role in that election. The Carter Administration's positions with respect to funding and management of R&D were fairly well-known by virtue of its having been in office for four years and having an articulate and effective spokesman in Frank Press.

There were few clues to what the Reagan Administration's policies might be. Reagan did have a science and technology brain trust. Sy Ramo and Art Bueche were the leading figures in it. Most of the members had long been associated with the Republican Patry and their lining up with Reagan was not unexpected. It is not clear, however, that they had much access to the inner circle during that period. Edward Teller was also involved, representing a fairly far right element in the science community.

Reagan was running on a platform in which he pledged to cut back the size of government. He had promised to eliminate the Department of Energy and the Department of Education. At the same time, there was discussion in both parties of increasing military spending, something which had already begun under the Carter Administration. Much was said, particularly on the Republican side, about deregulation, about eliminating regulatory agencies and "getting government off the back of the business community."

Very little was said about Reagan's views on basic research. One clue appeared in October, when Science magazine published an interview with Milton Friedman and his wife, Rose, conservative economists at the University of Chicago. The Friedmans were quoted as suggesting that in a conservative administration it might be appropriate to eliminate federal agencies which fund basic research such as the National Science Foundation and the National Institutes of Health, since support for basic research was more properly a responsibility of the private sector. It could be carried out by foundations and philanthropic organizations, as had been the case prior to World War II. That Science article, although it did not present any kind of official, authorized view, scared a lot of people in the scientific community, as might well be imagined.

Following the election a lot of changes did take place, of course, some of them very rapid. The original Reagan Administration science policy was not really a science policy at all. Rather it was an economic policy -- a budget policy -- applied to many areas, including science. That policy began to emerge in the form of the famous Stockman "Hit List," which was leaked to the press in the winter of 1980-81.

Just prior to leaving office, President Carter, as the law requires, presented his fiscal year 1982 budget to the Congress. The budget, of course, had no chance of being enacted and Carter chose to go out by presenting a budget which contained something for everyone. This gave the new administration many opportunities to make cuts, and cut they did -- eliminating everything that was new, virtually all new initiatives throughout the government, at least on the civil side. Beyond the initiatives, there were also deep cuts into the base in many agencies: in NSF, in the social sciences and science and engineering education; in the Department of Energy in alternative energy programs; and in EPA, in keeping with the emphasis on reducing the roles of regulatory agencies.

Two factors helped shape these choices. One was the pressure to cut government spending and to get the federal budget under control. The other was one of those broader currents, the changing view of the role of government in society.

It is important to note that these decisions and recommendations, although they had profound effects on science and R&D programs were made in general without the participation of scientific advisors. There is no indication that the transition team science advisors had much influence in shaping these choices. The decisions seem to have been made largely through the White House and OMB structure.

The President's science advisor, George Keyworth, did not come on board until late May. In many of the civilian agencies the assistant secretary slots (or their equivalents) were not filled until spring. In NSF, for example, where holdovers from the previous administration were in place throughout, they were simply not very well connected to the policymaking process. Many decisions on NSF were made without much participation on their part.

Perhaps most significant, though, is what did not happen. As you may have noticied, NSF and NIH were not eliminated, despite the threat that had been raised by the Friedmans' interview. And the government role in support of basic research, in fact, the government role in most areas of R&D was affirmed in the early budget statements, albeit in a relatively quiet way and with some variations on the previous administration's themes.

The formulation of an actual Reagan Administration science policy -- that is, a policy more carefully articulated and focused on that area of government and private sector activity, awaited the arrival on the scene of Keyworth. In terms of budgeting, that is, "policy for science," it is interesting to see how that policy has evolved. The most newsworthy item in Dr.

Keyworth's initial speech, a speech that set the tone for the early part of his tenure, was his proclamation that the United States should recognize that it cannot be first in everything. Keyworth noted that the nation must pursue excellence and relevance in its research -- not growth for its own sake. He suggested that the scientific community was going to have to learn to live with less.

Keyworth sought to distance himself from his predecessors in this manner. He also made known to the White House staff that he intended to be a policymaker for the administration and not an ambassador for the scientific community -- very important aspects of his subsequent success, I believe. As the administration's S&T policies have evolved, however, over the past several years they have tended to sound a good deal more like the policies of previous administrations than these initial volleys would have suggested. I think that is a function of the moderating influence of the scientific and technological communities, as exercised through OSTP, the R&D agencies and the Congress.

What are these policies in R&D funding? There have been sharp increases in military programs. These are mostly in the "D" (development) side of R&D. At the same time, there have been deep cuts in a number of civilian agencies, particularly in energy (applied research and development and demonstration programs in alternative energy sources) EPA, and NOAA. There was also an attempt to reduce the federal role in civilian aeronautical R&D, on the grounds this was more properly the job of the private sector.

That initiative was reversed through a process in which the aeronautics community was able to persuade decisionmakers in OMB that there was a very valuable role for the government in this area. Ideology apart, this was something the federal government had done very successfully and ought to continue to do. Civilian aeronautics is very important to our economy and our international trade position.

Finally -- and perhaps most surprising in retrospect -- funding for basic research has gone up rather substantially. The administration has given strong support to basic research, primarily in the physical sciences and mathematics and engineering. The life sciences have done reasonably well, also, although the administration has left the initiative in this area to the Congress and Congress has obliged by adding substantially to the amounts proposed for biomedical research in the annual budgets for the last several years. Even the social sciences, which were reduced very sharply in the initial round of budget cuts, have recovered somewhat. At least they have been brought back from the brink of extinction, and, with the help of Congress are regaining some of their former funding levels.

Let us look now at how these science and technology policies have been shaped by the broad current of politics and society. In the area of national security policy, as we have seen, defense R&D funding is up very sharply, in parallel with the overall increases in military spending. It is significant, of course, that the budget growth is in the D part -- or the DT&E elements -- of R, D, T&E. This is the part of the spectrum most closely associated with the immediate needs of military preparedness.

Also in the area of national security policy there has been a new and growing interest in exotic technologies: the Strategic Defense Initiative or the "Star Wars" program, as it is frequently called. The changes in defense R&D are the result of broader policy shifts: greater emphasis on national security as an area of policy, the fact that there are resources available, and the ascendency within the administration of enthusisasts for high-tech programs and high-tech solutions to national security problems.

At the same time, within the area of national security policy, there is a major thrust outside of the funding area. That is the growing concern over the flow of U.S. scientific and technical information to our military and political adversaries. More attention has been paid to this issue and there have been attempts to control the flow of information, attempts which some feel may come at the expense of progress in domestic science and productive international collaboration in technology.

Among the other currents affecting science is economics, the changing perceptions of our economic position. The Reagan Administration arrived on the scene in a period of double-digit inflation. R&D budgets were growing fairly well in nominal terms, but real growth was either very low or negative since inflation was eating up all of the increases. Inflation has been substantially reduced over the past three years. As a result, overall R&D funding and funding for basic research have been able to show significant real increases.

On the nondefense side, the overall budget for R&D has more or less held level. There has been a shift towards increasing basic research, while applied research and development on the civilian side have declined. That is actually a result of the confluence of the two currents: the economic situation and the changing view of the role of government. In any case, I think the economic situation has been something of a two-edged sword with respect to R&D policy during the current administration.

On one side, the need to control government expenditures because of economic conditions has exerted downward pressure on federal R&D spending because R&D programs represent controllable expenditures. On the other side, the economic situation has also served as something of a driving force with respect to growth in R&D programs. This is due to the increasing visibility and economic importance of high technology industries and of high technology imports (particularly from Japan). High technology is seen as the key to long-term economic success for this country and research, of course, is the key to high technology. So there is a two-edged sword operating with respect to economics.

Of course, the most important consequence of the economic situation may be yet to come. That is the matter of the federal budget deficit. In the past two years the budget process, both on the Congressional and Executive sides, has essentially ignored the deficit as a factor in economics and budgeting. Sooner or later that has got to change. We will return to that shortly.

The third broad current is the changing perception of the role of government -- the more restrictive view of what government ought to do -- that has been articulated by the current administration. This is the most ideology-bound of the three currents. Again this is not R&D policy per se, but it is responsible for the biggest shifts in civilian R&D, the termination of the big energy demonstration plants, and the reduction of R&D programs in several regulatory agencies.

In a perverse way, this more restricitive view of the role of government in society might account in part for the increased federal support of basic research in recent years. If research is seen as the key to high technology and high technology as the key to our economic salvation, then support of basic research by government may well be the most ideologically safe, consenual, and politically attractive type of action which government can take. It is something on which a conservative administration and more liberal Congress can agree. So, as tighter limits are placed on the role of government, the range of possible actions government may take to assist the economy is narrowed and increasing federal support for basic research becomes more and more attractive.

What does all this mean in terms of future R&D budgets and policies? Some people are talking in terms of a second round of massive changes, of another Stockman-type hitlist, assuming President Reagan is re-elected. This would mean massive reductions in federal expenditures following the elections.

The situation is different now than it was four years ago. In 1981 the Reagan Administration was new. The outgoing Carter Administration was the "establishment" and its budget was the establishment budget, that target. In 1984 the Reagan Administration is the establishment. Now, things could change, of course, depending on power shifts that might take place within the administration, within the White House staff and in the Executive Office. But barring massive shifts in the dramatis personae in the Executive Office, I do not think we are likely to see the same type of exercise as we did in 1981.

With respect to science and technology, there is also the fact that we have OSTP in place. (In 1981 there was some question as to whether the office would be retained by the incoming administration.) OSTP has now planted its feet strongly in national security policy and it has expertise in that area and the ability to assist the White House in policymaking with respect to a variety of important national security programs. At the same time, it serves -- despite Dr. Keyworth's efforts to maintain his independence -- as a channel of influence for the scientific establishment and as moderating force on policy that did not exist in 1981.

However, I am going to place one big qualification on all of this. The most important reality and social current is, of course, the budget deficit, which is currently running at about $200 billion per year. Despite the President's assertion that budget deficits have no relation to interest rates, the consensus of all economic wisdom in this country is that the budget deficit must be controlled or our economic recovery is doomed.

This deficit is going to need to be dealt with. It will probably have to be dealt with on the revenue side, but the government cannot raise taxes without cutting spending to make a tax increase politically acceptable. What this happens there is going to be strong pressure on those parts of the federal budget that are regarded as controllable.

Nondefense R&D programs in the current, fiscal 1985 budget total approximately $16 billion. Total controllable expenditures on the nondefense side of the budget total about $80 billion.

Nondefense R&D thus constitutes one-fifth of nondefense controllable government expenditures. It is hard to see how, in a climate of real fiscal austerity, despite all I have said about the politcal assets of science and technology, they can be immune from deep budget cuts.

DISCUSSION

DR. PFEIFFER: I am Heinz Pfeiffer from Pennsylvania Power and Light Company. I would like to ask Al, since he is connected with the AAAS, about another aspect of what I have seen as a change in science policy, which is a purely technical one, both in DOE, and especially organizations like SERI, that is a real tightening down on technical contents of the scientific programs that I think I have seen over the last four years, more of the judgments being made on scientific rather than social or political basis.

DR. TEICH: Well, I think that certainly in DOE and the example you cited, in SERI, that has been the case. Are you interested in my view as to whether that is a favorable or unfavorable development or my interpretation of why it is taking place?

DR. PFEIFFER: You have a broader view than I. I work with DOE and SERI and this has been an impression on my part and I wonder if you might agree or disagree on how broadly this occurs in program with which I am not familiar?

DR. TEICH: Well, I think there is a general orientation in the current administration to return to the harder sciences. That is reflected in the reductions in social science expenditures, as well as in the shift towards decision making on a more technical basis.

I think that what you see in DOE has, to a significant extent, been mirrored elsewhere in the government. I am not necessarily sure that it is entirely a favorable development. It is consistent with the Reagan Administration's policies of maintaining a focus on high-tech and staying away from some of the "softer" dimensions of social problems, seeking technical solutions rather than social solutions.

DR. CHERNICK: Cedric Chernick from the Searle Scholars Program. We seem for the first time during the last administration to have seen a politicization of appointments in the National Science Foundation. Do you think we are going to see an extension of this to all of the agencies or are we going to be able to maintain some of the apolitical nature?

DR. TEICH: Well, you know I think first of all, the politicization of appointments in NSF is probably less a factor than in some other agencies, Agriculture and the Department of Education being two cases in point. I think NSF is relatively free of that kind of thing, although some would contend that there is more than there was in the past.

113

I think what we are seeing really is a cost of the increasing imporance of science and research in society. When NSF was a small agency of a few hundred million dollars and science was viewed basically as something of interest to a bunch of professors in universities, nobody really cared that much about who was in charge of it and it could afford to be apolitical.

We see science now as the key to high-tech. It is much more visible. NSF has a billion and a half dollar budget. That is significant. It is relevant. A lot more congressmen know what NSF is and what it does. I think that is true also of research programs elswhere in the government. With increased influence and increased visiblity comes increased political interest and, therefore, increased political control.

I think that is just a natural evolution which might have some unfavorable dimensions, but it is a price one has to pay for increased influence.

DR. BARNES: Dennis Barnes, University of Virginia. Al, I just make one point to underscore what you said about assuming or believing that there would be a limited attack on research in the next administration.

I think there is one thing that is going to happen which will be different this time. The Senate, while Republican, will have a lot more folks up for reelection in '86 and I think one thing the Republicans have learned in this Senate in the last four years is it is not nearly as much fun to do away with programs as it is to add them. With so many of them up for reelection in '86, I think there is going to be a lot of resistance to their supporting any major cuts on the budget.

Although you sort of glossed over the prospect that there might be a Mondale Administration I would still like your impression. If there were a Mondale Administration, and in light of the obligations that administration might have to restoring social programs and in light of the major investments, rather good treament research has had in this administration, what would be your guesses about how that Mondale Administration would treat R&D?

DR. TEICH: First of all, I think there would be a reduction in the rate of growth of the military expenditures and military R&D as a portion of that. Again, that is part of not R&D policy specifically, but a function of the shift in priorities, although I think a Mondale Administration would still be committed to growth. There is pretty broad consensus on that on the military side.

I think on the civilian side you would see a considerable

114

pressure from the Democratic constituencies to increase spending in a variety of those softer areas of research which have been held back; that is, in education, in various of the smaller agencies then and the social sciences, probably in some areas of biomedical research, mental health and so on.

And I think that as a consequence of that, in view of the fiscal austerity which the Mondale Administration would face, just as a second Reagan Administration would, I think that would result probably in pressure to hold back on some programs in the physical sciences.

And I think, and I should have mentioned this earlier, that regardless of who wins, there are going to be some pressures on operational programs in the physical sciences and basic research because of the fact that we have taken on some fairly large mortgages for a number of construction projects, large, long-term, programs, accelerators in high energy physics, space stations, and so on.

Those programs have substantial run-out costs and they are going to cause some pressures on conduct on R&D in the physical sciences over the next several years. I think those pressures would be greater under a Mondale Administration because of the additional demands for increases in other realms.

DR. COOPER: Martin Cooper, Rohrback Technology. Al, you are an impartial observer of the Washington scene and when the Reagan Administration first came in they had very strong support and involvement, even prior to the formation of the administration, of industrialist corporate American helping to shape policy or at least having some input. Whether it was taken or not is another story, but at least they were involved.

What has happened in the past several years and do you see corporate America backing off these activities, maintaining them, increasing them, particularly within the R&D, not in terms of the capital side of the market, but in terms of its R&D pressures?

DR. TEICH: I may be stepping out on a limb here since here I am in the company of many people who are closer to this than I am, but I think that many leaders in the corporate world who are concerned about R&D have recognized that federal R&D policy, tax incentives and similar initiatives are more or less marginal with respect to their influence on private sector R&D funding.

I think these leaders may not be backing away, but I think they are recognizing this and putting it in proper perspective. This is not to say that federal policies as a whole, federal economic policies, do not have a major influence on the economy and, therefore, on R&D spending. But federal R&D policies themselves have not been the major influence.

I think what is happening -- and I see it as a favorable development -- is the growing recognition among corporation leaders of the importance of tightening the linkages, in terms of education and training of scientists and engineers. They are recognizing the need of the private sector to pay attention to what is going on in academia for the sake of their own future well being and because closer ties to universities can be valuable for <u>both</u> sides and not just a way for universities to get access to another source of R&D funding.

CHAPTER NINE
"Impacts on the Government: II"

Dr. Christopher Hill
Congressional Research Service

Introductory Remarks

DR. HAHN: We are next going to hear from Christopher Hill, Senior Specialist in Science and Technology at the Congressional Research Service. Chris has been around the circuit, like many of the people in this room and on the platform.

He used to be at the Uniroyal Research Labs, taught at Washington University, was a policy analyst at the Office of Technology Assessment and later at MIT in their Center for Policy Alternatives.

He is a well-known author to most of the people in this audience, who started out as a chem engineer and got his PhD from Wisconsin.

Now he is here back into government. I think the fact he has been in and out a few times gives him some unusual ability perhaps to see more clearly than some of us who stayed in the same places so long do not have. Chris.

DR. CHRISTOPHER HILL

Thank you, Walter. My remarks today are in two parts. First, I will review recent Congressional activities regarding science and technology. Then, I will offer my prepared remarks which analyze some of the central assumptions of modern science and technology policy. Let me begin by associating myself with the vast majority of Al Teich's remarks.

I would have said almost the same thing about the background and climate for R&D, the historical perspective on the last four years, the pressures on and responses of the R&D system, the attitudes with which the administration came into office, the learning that went on, the reassessment of its political positions, and the adjustments it made.

There is, of course, no mystery, having listened to Al, in understanding where the U-shaped curves that characterized Charlier Falk's presentation came from. They came from that initial period in the administration when it appeared that we

117

were doing far too much in science and from the later recognition that science offered a great deal more opportunity and that we ought to get back into a number of things that we initially started out of.

Let me observe that, probably quite independent of any ideological position or intention, the expenditures of the federal government on what I call "investment programs" have declined sharply during the last four years, as compared with the levels of similar expenditures during the previous 20 years.

I recently did an exercise in which I aggregated federal expenditure programs, that make investments in plant and equipment, in human capital, and in research and development. These included both defense and civilian programs in such areas as R&D, defense construction, airport, highway, and post construction, education, child nutrition and so on.

I found our commitment to investment activities, which was remarkably constant both as a fraction of GNP and fraction of the total federal budget over the previous 20 years, has dropped sharply during the Reagan Administration. Based on the official budget projections, it continues to drop sharply into the next few years.

This is a significant indicator of the administration's revealed priorities, even if it has nothing to do with a position taken in advance, but only reflects how things work out.

OVERVIEW OF RECENT CONGRESSIONAL INTEREST IN R&D

More than 300 pieces of legislation were introduced in the 98th Congress, about to conclude, on the subject of technology, innovation and science. This suggests that Congress as an institution is very interested in technology. Of course, the vast majority of these bills are looking for ways to take advantage of technology, not to regulate and control it.

Over the last couple of years a number of bills have been passed, most of which we have talked about here already. The R&D tax credit we discussed yesterday was passed as part of the Reagan Administration's 1981 Economic Recovery Tax Act. The Small Business Research Act we discussed yesterday was passed in 1982.

More recently, a Math and Science Education Bill, which provides nearly half a billion dollars a year of authorization for funding in the Department of Education and the NSF for elementary and secondary education programs in the math and science area was passed.

Just two weeks ago, the National Cooperative R&D Act was passed. It has not yet been signed into law, but every expectation is that it will be. The act provides certain antitrust relief related to the level of damages, standards of proof, and so on, in antitrust actions against cooperative R&D ventures among firms in an industry. It is not the intent of this bill that everyone in the industry get together to do research. The conference committee report on the bill is quite clear that this bill is not to be interpreted to give license for all the firms to get together. It wants to see at least four competing bodies in any field of technology. Any activity that looks like it would reduce the number of competitors below four is probably not going to be allowed, except in special cases.

The Patent Term Restoration bill for new pharmaceuticals whose period of effective patent coverage is reduced by regulatory review was passed as part of a trade-off to get generic drug legislation passed.

Recently, the NSF act amendment which puts engineering on an equal footing with the sciences in the charter of the National Science Foundation was passed in both houses. It is not yet clear whether it will be signed into law, but I expect that it will be.

As part of the same package, the Congress passed the Manufacturing Sciences and Robotics R&D Act. Its major feature is a new program in the Department of Commerce to support research, development and technology transfer activities in advanced manufacturing and robotics, computer-aided design, flexible manufacturing and so on.

This bill illustrates an important point about the congressional response to science policy initiatives: Congress imposes its own institutional constraints on what happens . Some have argued that the manufacturing bill assigns new responsibilities for supporting research and development to the Commerce Department, not because the Commerce Department is a good place to put such activity, but because for the last four years the Senate has not passed an authorization bill for the National Science Foundation due to a jurisdictional tussle between two committees. So as long as it is not possible to pass an NSF authorization, one must find creative ways to start new things.

Other bills that were considered, but not passed are also of interest. Congressman LaFalce introduced an Advanced Technology Foundation bill, which would have set up a new independent agency similar to NSF to support applied research related to industrial technology and to fund and coordinate state programs of industrial extension. This bill did not receive a lot of

119

attention, but it did get favorable vote in the House Banking Committee in April of this year on essentially a party line basis, with one Democrat voting against it.

Similarly, the National Technology Foundation proposal of Congressman Brown was again considered in the House Science and Technology Committee. That bill, along with the Advanced Technology Foundation bill, were not acted on by the Science and Technology Committee and, in the parlance, died there. Whether they will be resurrected remains to be seen.

As you know, Congress did not pass the R&D tax credit extension. And, if you believe the scenario Al Teich laid out for us, it is almost impossible to imagine that next year Congress could make the R&D tax credit permanent or do anything else to provide additional subsidy for industry in a period when we may see major tax increase and/or major budget cutbacks. I could be wrong, but I suspect that it has little chance.

During the last few years Congress has acted on a number of ideas related to the climate for innovation, including proposals that have been floating around for 15 or 20 years. Many of the proposals passed during this last session, such as antitrust relief, patent term restoration, and the R&D tax credit go back to the Charpie Report of 1967, or earlier. As of now, the agenda of changing the climate for innovation is reasonably well played out.

With the exception of the R&D tax credit, it is difficult to imagine consideration of another set of initiatives related to making the climate for R&D better in the next Congress.

One does not ordinarily see an interest group simply disappear when they get what they want: they come up with new things to want. I am curious about what interests that are concerned for industrial innovation will do next. Do they feel they now have what they want? Will they come back with a new package? Will there be some new ideas, and how will they play out politically?

Let me mention two or three other things that Congress is involved in that have not become legislation at this time, but may become so.

One of the interesting things that happened during the last 18 months or so was that both parties in both houses of Congress set up study groups that produced documents stating their positions on what the government should do to take advantage of new technology. However, those reports have not yet stimulated much action. In some cases they have reaffirmed the party's positions, while others have staked out new positions that have not yet been developed into legislation or for which the

120

legislation has not gone forward.

It will be interesting to see what becomes of these reports in the future: whether they will simply disappear like most other reports, or the investments made in them will lead to new initiatives in the next congress.

There is another interesting development just beginning. A coalition of a number of the special caucuses in the Congress, including the Congressional Clearing House on the Future, the Sunbelt Caucus, the Northeast-Midwest Coalition, is joining with the Business and Higher Education Forum to develop a working relationship and perhaps later a program or a set of proposals on R&D policy. The folks involved in that on the congressional side are activitists who want changes made. So it will be interesting to see how that goes.

John Holmfeld mentioned yesterday that the House Committee on Science and Technology has set up a new task force which intends to take a comprehensive look at the whole question of our nation's science policy over the next two years. Exactly where this will lead is not clear. The chairman of the committee says his objective is "To educate the members about science policy," and we will see where such education might take us in terms of action.

DISCUSSION

DR. STEVENSON: Jim Stevenson, Georgia Tech. There have been a number of initiatives recently by universities that scientific societies have said bypass the peer review process. Congress, on the other hand, says, well, there is an added dimension, economic development, and peer review has no basis for judging these things. Do you see in the future an increasing amount of separate initiatives coming along?

DR. HILL: You are, of course, referring to what was uncharitably called pork barrel science yesterday. That is not really the domain to which I intend my remark to be directed.

Let me say that my comments about peer review have to do more with project-level funding, where so many investigators spend so much time chasing after the next grant that they can never do a good job on what they are doing. I see a growing interest in trying to get some of that pressure off so investigators can devote more attention to doing good research.

With respect to the question of where large scale facilities get located, John made the point very well, science is in the big leagues now. Others have made the point that this kind of activity is going on because there has been a long period of perhaps inadequate support for facilities construction. However, the recent Congressional actions have brought the facilities issue to the fore, and it may be that, subject to budget constraints, something will be done about the facilities problem to take some of the pressure off. However, I suspect that we will see a continuing stream of special provisions for specific facilities.

DR. WALKER: Eric Walker from Penn State. I must commend you on how well, how assiduously and almost perfectly you avoided the word "engineering" until your last paragraph.

You know, we engineers have developed an inferiority complex because you avoid us this way. Originally when the National Science Foundation Act was passed it had the word "engineering" in it. But the wave then was we get out of war work, we get out of practical things and go back to basic science and the word "engineering" was stricken from the act.

The National Science Foundation, when first formed, was almost a foundation for the support of physics, chemistry and perhaps mathematics. And it was to be an independent foundation that the federal government could give money to. Industry could also contribute and foundations could contribute, but eventually it became a captive of the federal government and almost its only source of support was the federal government funds and it was run by physicists, chemists and mathematics people.

I once had one of my professors say to me, "You know, we only do pure research and my research is so pure that nobody will ever find a use for it."

Gradually we have come around to think of research and development -- and you say that as one word -- I would like to think of them as being two words. Research is finding new knowledge, development is putting it to work, and that is the job of the engineers.

And I note a sort of resurgence on the part of the engineers wanting to be recognized. It is pretty hard when the National Science Foundation talks about scientists and engineers as if S comes before E in the alphabet, and in spite of the fact there are ten times as many engineers as there are scientists, but we also talk about scientists and engineers.

The AAAS, you know, is now going through a procedure whereby they are saying maybe we should add engineering to our title, AAA, Science and Engineering.

I think if we recognize in this business that engineering is putting this basic knowledge to work, and that is what the administration is trying to do, to get some more benefits for mankind or benefits for the country by the fact that we are not all scientists.

You may call us engineers, you may call us technologists, but the job is to put all of this knowledge to work for the benefit of the country.

I am very hopeful that there is going to be more emphasis on this end of science and technology. I just wonder, do you see this sort of wave coming? Maybe I should ask this of a futurist.

DR. HILL: I would have to agree with most of Professor Walker's comments and observations on the situation.

From where I sit, the engineering community does not appear to have a very clear sense of the problem it faces and how it might address it. A couple of things about the engineering position strike me as rather peculiar.

It seems to me that if one wanted to strengthen the federal support for research related to engineering, that one might not put quite so much effort into trying to bend the National Science Foundation in that direction, there might be a better strategy.

I find peculiar the absolute lack of interest on the part of the engineering community in any of the other initiatives related to new organizations, new structures, or new programs in support of applied research and technology. I see more hostility than support, and I do not understand that position in terms of what I perceive to be the engineers' political interest. The NSF battle, it seems to me, is ultimately a lost cause. Of course, the NSF people here might disagree.

I would observe further that support for basic research in engineering in universities is not the same as concern about technology. To the extent that we base our engineering research in universities on the NSF basic sciences project grant model, we may not be doing much for technology by supporting basic research in engineering through that mechanism. So, I do not understand the engineering community perspective on these matters.

DR. YOUNG: Leo Young. I have finally been provoked. Having participated a little bit in the change in the NSF that took place when an engineering directorate was set up, working through the IEEE and AAAS, at this time I do not think the NSF is a lost cause.

As I see it, science and engineering needs to be brought together. There was discussion at the time, including with George Brown, of the possibility of setting up a separate national engineering foundation which would be separate from the National Science Foundation.

I personally opposed that concept because I felt science and engineering had to work together and it should be within one single foundation. In fact, it resulted in the change in the NSF which took place in 1980 or 1981 of setting up a separate directorate, which was called the Engineering Directorate.

We saw this as a step in the right direction, but the war still had not been won. We may lose the war, but I still think this is a good chance that NSF will, in fact, recognize that engineering and science are equal partners, if you will.

The same kind of thing happened in the National Academy of Sciences, where you have the National Academy of Engineering now moving up in the world, not as fast as some people would like, but it is moving up and it has become an equal partner with science. Unless we move in that direction I think the country as a whole is a loser. So I am optimistic on the changes.

DR. HILL: Of course, we all have great hopes that you are correct. I remember applying for basic research grants in engineering when I was an engineering faculty member. The programs at NSF to which I applied in 1971 or 1972 are the same programs that are there today, directed by the same program managers. And I have yet to be able to understand how the creation of an engineering directorate two or three years ago has made any substantive difference in the NSF organization. The same people are running the same programs, using the same review procedures, the same mailing lists, the same reviewers, and the same culture of decision that was there all through the Nineteen-seventies. I do not see that there has been a change in anything but the words on the door.

I think that it is also important to realize that, at least in terms of discussions on Capitol Hill, most people still talk about the "Academy of Sciences," and NAE, despite its distinguished 20 year history, has not yet managed to establish an independent identity.

DR. WALKER: I make one more comment about that. I was Chairman of the National Science Board at the time we tried to form a division of engineering. The board voted we should have a division of engineering and nothing happened for one year. When I asked the director what had happened to the division of engineering he said, "Oh, I did not think the board meant it."

One other anecdote. I was also, as you probably know, the President of the National Academy of Engineering. And the biggest mistake I made as the President of the National Academy of Engineering was not to separate from the National Academy of Sciences. We did not do it because so many of our members said you cannot separate science and engineering. I still say we should have separated.

DR. GAMOTA: George Gamota from the University of Michigan. I would like to point out there is a major need in the country for engineering research and one of my concerns is the ultimate decision for budget is made by people who really understand very little more about engineering or research or science.

If you have an organization that exists and you suddenly say this organization needs 50, 60 maybe 100 percent increase in budget because there is another responsibility, I think it is wishful thinking that is going to pass through the budget.

A separate agency, on the other hand, given life can, in fact, be given substantial funding over and above.

My concern is ultimately, whoever wins in November, there is going to be tremendous pressure keeping each organization at a certain level. Engineering research certainly equals the needs of that of science and so given it altogether, I predict that engineering research will grow much less than what is needed and, in fact, at the expense of science. This is a major need, you need to figure out how to get a new organization like NIH. NIH could have been born out of NSF, but if it was, it would have never grown to the size it has today. I think it is food for thought.

DR. HAHN: Let me close with just a few quick remarks. I am not going to give you a speech, but let me give you the bullets of a couple of points on impacts on government of the Reagan science policy activities that come from a different viewpoint.

One is this administration looks like it is flying blind while operating on VFR rules. There is very little sensing of future environments of any kind and very little "visioning," as some of the people call it, of either one or a range of alternative futures.

A lot of their science policy stems from ideology. This has already been observed in practice in economics and in other social areas that are given or denied priorities in attention and in budgets. I am not arguing with the priorities -- this is just an observation on behavior.

Where the administration should find itself at a disadvantage is that it is surrounded by forward-looking activities, "looking out the windshield" is my phrase for them.

For example, on Capitol Hill the Congressional Clearing House on the Future and its nonprofit Institute, is one pair. The Congressional Science and Technology Caucus, with its brand new Research Institute for Space, Science and Technology which was just started last Tuesday has a charter that asks long range questions and focuses on looking forward. The industries that implement much of this research and development are engaging in activities called foresight and issues management. They are sensing the environment out a couple of business cycles ahead of where they are and determining what the impact of alternative futures -- undesirable ones and desirable ones -- might be and how they affect their business.

There is an organization called the Issues Management Association which grew up in the last two years. IMA has 500 people, mostly in industry, who are doing this environmental scanning rather systematically.

So the Administration finds itself in an environment where universities like my own, many industrial activities like these represented here, numerous people on Capitol Hill, many of the voluntary sector groups, particularly the environmentalists, are all looking forward in various and sundry ways. They are using the techniques that scientists and engineers, hard and soft, have given them while the administration sits in its darkness. This

126

has its hazards for all of us.

Another point is we that do not communicate because of government, industry, academic and voluntary sector barriers. We each seem to have our own cultures and languages. The basic research scientists are still defending their freedom of pursuit of research, they do not understand the engineers and engineers are getting very uptight. The budgeteers, the economists and politicians do not understand any of the S&T types but know they are on top.

And, of course, the lawyers sit there smugly collecting fees we all envy while the whole milieu churns on in no particular direction! Our localized values and attitudes inhibit constructive conversation.

Ian Ross asked the key question in the keynote: Where is the forum? We do not have a forum. We have lots of voices. We have not bridged these sector barriers. One of the challenges to us -- and maybe to NCAR -- is how to start. How can we in forums like this begin to understand and talk to each other? Even if we do not like what "they" say, it might be better if we could do better at listening.

CHAPTER TEN
"Comments on the Group Disccusions"

Dr. Gamota
University of Michigan

As I went around to the five sessions this morning, some burning issues emerged; some of them may turn out to be real "sleepers". One of the things that sort of hits me is that as you go around the country, every state, every region, almost down to the county size, has a research park going.

Every governor I know has a commission on high-tech and plans to emulate Silicon Valley or Route 128.

And as you sit back you have to wonder, particularly in the political world that we live in, when the accounting is going to come. For two or three years, maybe a maximum of four years, people are willing to provide support for high-tech to the scientists and engineers, but as the saying goes, "Where's the beef?" It has to come through sooner or later, and in many cases it will probably be sooner.

We here at NCAR should think about it. Certainly not all of the things that are being said in the name of science or high-tech can succeed. Every single state and region in this country is not going to have a mini Silicon Valley.

In preparing for the majority of those initiatives not succeeding, what can we do to ensure that, in fact, the successes outweigh the negatives; and what can we do, in fact, to make sure there are adequate successes and that these are well publicized.

It is always nice to get more dollars into your own research programs and we are delighted with that, but the fact of the matter is that we need support on a long-term basis -- and we should remember, long-term means more than four years. Our goal is to ensure that society continually sees the benefits of science and technology. It must be a good investment on a long-term basis with visible signs every once in a while.

So I would like to open up the dialogue and hear some of your thoughts about what we can do during the next two to four years to ensure the investment society is making now pays off -- and it is making it. Whether you are at a university or in industry or government, everybody's betting on high-tech. How can we, in fact, make sure those investments are going to pay. The net result must be more than the negative offsets.

Taking an example from the past, as you remember back in the early 1970's we were going to have a cure for cancer in two

128

years. Well, we still do not have it. There have been some successes, but people clearly are questioning some of the investments we have been making to prolong life and wondering whether, in fact, it is worth it. In high-tech, the bill is also going to come.

I know in my own state, in Michigan, there is a lot of betting on it. I worry whether or not we will be able to deliver. Diversification into high-tech is good, but it will not replace the automobile business nor should people expect it to.

Let me remind you that back in the 1970's and even in the 1960's everybody thought science was the panacea, and every single industrial laboratory set up an R&D organization.

Then, starting with a few major companies there was a slaughter or R&D organizations where major companies just sort of removed their R&D arms, one after the other. In New Jersey it was really a blood bath. The Air Force removed some of its laboratories also as you might remember. I am worried that if we do not plan the next stage, this euphoria might be short lived.

Another point raised at several of the discussion groups was the question of the funding gap between applied research or technology that seems to be developing in the U.S. due to the administration policy that government should support only basic research whereas civilian applied research and development should be picked up by industry.

Bruce Merrifield, who is the Assistant Secretary for Commerce for productivity, has a slide showing this technological gap which he says he's going to fill with such initiatives as industrial cooperatives. Semiconductor Research Cooperative, is one that he cited, and of course, another one is the MCC in Austin, Texas, that Bobby Inman runs.

The question is, do you feel that such cooperatives can build up momentum and take up that developing gap? To me that gap is very large. It is anywhere between a minimum of $10 to $30 billion.

The chemical industry tried to do this a couple years ago and to a large degree failed, mainly due to lack of agreement within industry itself. But applied research is critical to our success as a nation. It the government does not pay for it and industry does not support it, then our fruits of basic research will be applied by our technological competitors in Japan, Europe and the Soviet Union.

Commerce is funding a program I am somewhat involved in that is looking at the Japanese science and technology, and

129

preliminary results are very interesting. The Japanese have targeted a number of areas, which is no surprise, but they have also evaluated the state of U.S. science and technology in those areas and invest in those in which we do poorly. In others they wait for our results.

They are looking at basic research, applied research, development and commercialization. Interestingly enough, in those areas where we are weaker, like basic research in manufacturing, they are substantially funding it to offset our weakness. In areas where we have a lot of money in basic research, they have cut back on their own support and are totally dependent upon us.

CHAPTER ELEVEN
"A Gubernatorial Perspective"

Governor Robb
The Commonwealth of Virginia

I am delighted to bring you, somewhat belatedly, greetings.

I have been working very closely with Dennis Barnes, and, whatever modest statement he may have made about the Continuous Electron Beam Accelerator Facility, it has been his leadership, both here and in the Congress and elsewhere, that has assisted us in keeping the project very much on track. Jim McCarthy of the University of Virginia is providing the scientific leadership for the project, but Dennis is working (administratively) with our office and many others to bring about the kind of a cooperative partnership which is probably as well represented by this gathering as any other that we have had in the Commonwealth.

That was the real reason I wanted to stop by. I was over this morning dedicating a new Nissan facility in the Port of Hampton Roads and was helicoptering back and was happy to stop. I did not realize that helicopter landing would stop the coed activities at the College of William and Mary as we landed on the soccer field, and I regret that I will probably be very unpopular after they find out who it was.

In any event, in both the CEBAF project with SURA -- in which Dennis has been so directly and effectively involved for such a long time -- and in the Center for Innovative Technology -- about which you have heard, I hope, and about which you will hear more -- we are very excited about what is happening. They are prime examples of (governmental) opportunities to participate with the community of scholars and of research and development in business.

I appreciate the fact that federal participants are part of your equation. I wish you well as one who has urged the federal government in many other areas to cut back -- or restrict funding -- to balance the federal government to do more for the long-term interests of us all.

Had I been more successful in my original pursuit of science I might have been able to go where Dennis was trying to lead me. Unfortunately I went astray, got into business, (then) law, (then) politics, and have not been able to hold a steady job for more than four years at a time since, even in the military.

I enjoy interacting with the community represented by those of

131

you here today, and I bid you welcome to the Commonwealth of Virginia. It is our hope that CEBAF and CIT may arouse your intellectual curiosity and that you will find opportunities to enjoy the amenities and quality of life here.

Let me just say that the Center for Innovative Technology is very much on course at this time, and that we are close to announcing the president of that organization. Research institutes are already operating at the University of Virginia, Virginia Polytechnic and State University and Virginia Commonwealth University. CEBAF comes along on schedule and attracts the kind of world class researchers and produces the spinoffs that we hope, a research institute would be created at the College of William and Mary for high energy physics, in addition to the other institutes.

I understand that a visit to NASA Langley is one of your options this afternoon, along with tennis and golf. The weather is beautiful today, so you may have a very difficult choice to make. I am sure you will choose wisely.

I welcome all of you to Virginia. I hope you have a very pleasant stay and that you and your families will want to return, perhaps for the professional opportunities we expect to be reinforcing and developing here within the Commonwealth of Virginia.

Thank you very much for permitting me literally to drop in and welcome you. Thank you for choosing Williamsburg, and please come back to visit us.

Thank you.

INTRODUCTORY REMARKS
"Impacts on Universities"

Don I. Phillips
Government-University-Industry Research Roundtable

Introductory Remarks

DR. HOGAN: This morning marks our final session on impacts.
This morning we will be looking at the federal policy impacts on
the university. Once again we hope we have assembled a very fine
panel to share their thoughts with you. That will be followed by
a summary.

This morning's session is going to be chaired by Don Phillips,
who   is   the   Executive   Director   of   the
Government-University-Industry Research Round Table. First I am
going to ask Don if he will tell you a little bit about the Round
Table because you may not have the complete background and the
details of this organization.   Then he will introduce his
speakers. Don.

DR. DON PHILLIPS

Thank you. Good morning. The Round Table has been mentioned
a few times so I will say a few words about that and move quickly
into the program, which is the reason we are all here.

The Round Table is a new unit sponsored by the Council of the
National Academy of Sciences. It was established in response to
recommendations coming out of two major committees; one, the
National Commission on Research, which existed between 1978 and
1980 and was concerned with the problems and tensions between the
government and universities, and the follow-on to that committee,
the Ad Hoc Committee on Government-University Relations in
support of Science, of the National Academy of Sciences, that
issued its report in 1982.

Both of these groups concluded that the types of issues and
problems that need to be addressed can not be dealt with
adequately by a committee with a finite lifetime issuing one or
more reports and then disbanding and going home. There needs to
be some continuing presence, preferably some neutral ground,
where the principals can come together on an on-going basis to
consider the problems and opportunities important to American
science.   This idea was translated into what has become the
Government-University-Industry Research Round Table at the
National Academy of Sciences.

133

I will quickly run through the Round Table. The Round Table is guided by a Council made up of 18 members, including the senior federal R&D officials -- the President's Science Advisor, Directors of NSF, NIH, Energy Research and Defense Research -- senior university officials, working scientists from university and industry and senior industrial officials.

The purpose of the Council is to establish the agenda based on input from individuals from all sectors and to be the guiding force in the operation of the Round Table.

In addition, we are establishing four working groups to examine and elucidate particular issues in greater depth. One is concerned with the question of talent: How do you get good people into science and engineering on an ongoing basis? The second is called, "Capacity of Academic Science and Engineering: Institutional Renewal," and is concerned with the physical infrastructure of universities, with improving the relationships between the sponsors and performers of research, and with means to more effectively supporting and conducting multidisciplinary research.

The third group, "New Alliances and Partnerships: Enhancing the Utilization of Scientific Advances," is concerned with the relationship between academic science, small and big business, federal labs, and state government.

The fourth group, the least well-defined at the moment, is concerned with major issues underlying the operation of the scientific enterprise. Two of the Council members, Harold Shapiro, the president of the University of Michigan, and Ed Jefferson, the CEO of DuPont, are working on a background paper to raise some of the questions that the group might address.

Two final points: first, the Round Table is intended to be an open shop, not a closed shop. We seek to involve as many individuals and organizations in the deliberations as have an interest in the problems and opportunities. Second, the Round Table was set up as an alternative to the traditional type of committee that is often constituted to address these issues. Thus it is easy to say what we are not. It is more difficult to say what we are.

Everyone agrees on the goals, everyone has been anxious to participate in the activities of the Council and the working groups. We still have some way to go, however, to decide what activities, procedures, and approaches will be most effective in achieving the goals.

The plan for the morning is to start off with two speakers, Dr. Robert Barker and Dr. Bill Risen. Then we will have our senior academic officer have the final word, as they are accustomed to doing.

In light of the remarks that Mary Good made earlier in the week, it is noteworthy that on this panel we have an honest-to-goodness working scientist. I see, unfortunately, that he has an administrative title among his current responsibilities, but that is minor. His major responsibility is a practicing chemist, so we will have an opportunity to get the views of a day-to-day working scientist.

We will start off, however, with Dr. Robert Barker, who is currently Provost at Cornell University. He has been a Vice-President for Research there and Director of their Division of Biological Sciences. He has also been a productive working scientist at several other institutions, including Tennessee, Iowa, Michigan State and Cornell.

One of his recent responsibilities at Cornell has been to lead the establishment of a unique university-industry-government partnership in basic biotechnology. In addition, he has been involved in some of the activities in which Cornell has had some unique experiences, some pleasant, perhaps some unpleasant, in the area of scientific control of scientific communication. It is some of those experiences, among others, that he will share with us this morning.

CHAPTER TWELVE
"Impacts on Universities: I"

Dr. Robert Barker
Cornell University

This is for me an interesting meeting. It brings together three cultures that are interested and involved in research in this country, the universities, industries and government. There are not too many forums in which these groups can come together and talk about the interactions and intersections between their three cultures.

What I want to do today is talk about these intersections, particularly where there may be some friction.

My interest in the general subject of how university, industry and government can collaborate, began about four years ago. At that time I sensed great tension between some of the collaborators.

I particularly refer to a meeting I attended that involved CEO's of about six or seven corporations who had been invited to the Cornell campus to talk about university-industry collaboration. Their general perception, which was talked about at great length, was that most university basic research was a waste of time and money.

Descriptors used in that session included some that used to be traditional in talking about the universities. Such words as "Ivory Tower and Egghead."

I find that more recently what used to be called the Ivory Tower is now a crumbling educational infrastructure and a matter of great concern to the nation. What used to be called an egg head is now looked to as a person who may drive the engine of economic recovery.

That may be an overstatement, but at least there has been a definite change and the "traditional" terms I have used have essentially disappeared. I'm pleased that we don't hear them much any more.

I want to start by talking a little about the role of states in relationship to the development of science in this country. The states have long had a role. They have built at their own expense many of the research universities that we currently look to for economic development, and within the last four or five years almost every state has taken on fresh initiatives to try to use the universities as instruments for economic redevelopment.

This increased interest on the part of the states requires the research universities be alert to what their state is doing to initiate programs in which the state, the university and industry can come together to stimulate economic growth.

This produces for the universities a diversity of opportunities that did not exist before. But there is a down side because many of the state programs have a rather short-term view. The states, to some degree, have adopted what we have blamed -- I am not sure entirely correctly -- industry for in the past; taking a short-term view as to what will pay off.

There has been quite a lot of discussion of this matter in New York State and there is debate at the moment between the seven universities that have been designated by the state as Centers for Advanced Technology and the Science and Technology Foundation of the state which is responsible for that program. The debate centers on how short a view should be taken to judge the success of those programs.

We were asked, for example, after six months what indicators pointed to the economic development had that occurred because the state had so far given us something of the order of $400,000 for research and development in biotechnology.

The state is also having influences on science policy and the universities in other ways. Many states are taking on responsibilities for such traditional federal responsibilities as health and safety and similar matters that they did not pay much attention to before.

For example, New York State has passed a law called the Right to Know Law. It requires that an employer be able to respond to an employee's inquiry about the toxic effects of a material with which they may come in contact.

It is an interesting law because it does not define exposure and has not created a list of toxic substances. So there are at least two big unknowns and the employer has something of the order of 72 hours in which to respond or the person can walk off the job.

The reason that this law is significant to universities becomes apparent if you think about the range of toxic substances that exist in universities and you think of what might constitute exposure, you can realize the dimension of the problem. I am not speaking against the law, it is well motived.

However, for the universities, particularly Cornell, it has

required a lot of effort, which ultimately will be to the good, but which has redirected some of the university's resources away from the business of teaching and research toward meshing with and even helping to form the regulations which the state is developing.

I am sensitive to this because we were the first institution (educational or otherwise) in the state to be required to develop educational programs and response programs. Fortunately, these will be made available by Cornell to other institutions in the state.

The next thing I want to mention is a state policy change that might not on the surface seem to affect the role of universities in pursuing research and science.

The State of New York last year passed a law which gave those state employees who had 20 years of service and who wished to retire an extra three years of retirement benefits if they did it within a three month period. A similar opportunity is available this year.

The outcome of that was Cornell University had 56 retirements, 40 of which were faculty. The effect on our ability to deliver on our programs was immediate. Some effects were definitely negative. Some of the faculty who could retire and to whom the program looked attractive were the better paid, the more successful ones, and the more important to the university mission.

The good effect has been, and it may have been inadvertent, that as we rehire, at a junior level, we can redirect our research and teaching programs. In addition, our age distribution was such that the retirement plan fitted with what we needed to do to establish a better age distribution among faculty.

What I am pointing out here is that the policies of the state, even though they are not aimed directly at the universities, can and do have substantial effects on the universities and upon the university's ability to pursue its major missions.

I would draw particular attention to the fact that the states' initiatives with regard to economic development have a shorter time line than do federal programs. I think the reason for that may be that most governors do not see themselves staying in office. They need a short time line so they can point to the success of their programs.

I am going to switch now to consideration of federal policies. I want to touch briefly on indirect costs. The subject is going to be brought up again in the next presentation.

It seems to me within the federal government there is conflict between the various elements of the federal government that deal with indirect costs.

The policy set by the Congress requires that the government pay full costs of research in the universities. That policy does not seem to be very well understood by the people who actually implement the programs that provide research funds to the universities.

Different agencies have different attitudes and the people who administer grants and contracts at agencies like NSF often resent the assessment of indirect costs. I would also if I were in their shoes, since to the extent that they pay indirect costs they do not seem to be getting a return for the research dollars spent.

It seems to me that within the federal government it would be to everyone's advantage if there could be developed a shared understanding of what the indirect cost system is all about. Part of the problem lies in the fact that virtually none of the administrators in the federal agencies have had administrative experience in a research university that would provide a perspective on that side of the indirect cost issue.

It is interesting to me also that when we deal with industry we often find they do not want to pay indirect costs either.

Now, the indirect costs in universities have escalated substantially, a matter of legitimate concern.

However, when I talk to colleagues in industry what their indirect cost rates are, they exceed ours substantially, as do those in the national laboratories.

I do not think it is a fact that indirect cost rates are too high. It is just that the indirect cost dollar is coming out of the same pocket that holds the dollars directly spent for research and indirect costs appear to diminish the research budget.

There are a good number of reasons, in my view, why indirect costs have gone up. We at the university have had to install a whole variety of new "systems." All of them have some impact.

We have personnel systems, health and human safety systems, a large number of reporting requirements, and extensive and complex accounting for research expenditures to name only a few.

139

We have the cost of renovation of facilities and, recently, everybody who provides instrumentation wants that to be done with cost sharing. For example, if NSF gives a dollar you have to find another dollar from some other donor. The same thing goes to some degree with industry. Often we find ourself able to get a dollar from one agency and then having to spend time to find the matching dollar from another one.

There is a relationship of this to the increase in indirect costs. To the extent the university puts its own or industry's funds into instrument purchases, the cost is added to the indirect cost recovery system. So, these agency policies are pushing up indirect costs because of an unwillingness to meet the full cost of instrumentation as a direct cost. That is the way it works!

I do not blame the people who are in grants management, as I said, for their attitudes. Most of them have not been in the university in settings where they can look at the system as a whole. I have to tell you, I have studied it carefully for a year and I am still not sure I understand it, but I do think we need to aim for a better understanding of what indirect costs are and perhaps arrive at some resolution of how to deal with it.

Finally I want to talk a little of the policy area I am supposed to talk about, that is scientific communication and national security.

There is a rather large book which is referred to in short as the Corson Report, which came out of a committee study of this matter and was published about a year ago.

The reason for concern here is again that there seems to be a conflict between two elements of our culture.

One is the element which is concerned with national security and, with full justification, wishes to protect us from the flow of information to those who we perceive may be our enemies, to protect us from a flow of information which would increase their capabilities for armaments and defense.

The other is the element of the university research community that is involved in activities that create or use the same kind of information. The conflict arises because most universities operate as fully open institutions in which all information can be shared.

In the case of Cornell University, it is part of the institutional culture and the principle is very strongly held to that the university must be open. And that means open, not just to members of the United States society, but to all societies. It

140

also means access is not determined by concern for our national security.

There has been very recently a resolution of what a year ago was a major conflict. The conflict sharpened when the Department of Defense indicated that it would take upon itself the identification of certain research that might be done in a university as "sensitive." If a project was sensitive the university had to be able to sequester it from access by foreign nationals who had not previously been cleared by the Department of Defense.

That meant that if the university was involved in research sponsored by DOD, that agency might, after the fact, declare the work to be sensitive and thereafter the university would have to limit access to it.

When the university community looked at that, it appeared that such work would fall within our definition of secret. Now it turns our "secret" has been defined by Congress and secret in the universities' terms is not secret in the federal government terms. So part of the difficulty in this area has been the taxonomy, understanding what the words mean.

Cornell got very involved because one of our faculty received a request to pursue research in an area that had to do with gallium arsenide. The contract which we were sent differed substantially from ones which we had received before, in that it required us to only employ foreign nationals who were cleared by DOD on the project. In addition, it would have limited us from publication even to the extent of holding seminars within the institution.

And further, it would have required us to guarantee that unapproved foreign nationals would not have access to the work which was being done, this in a department where there were 35 foreign graduate students and postdoctorals, of whom only a small number would have been cleared to be involved in the project.

By definition we would have had to set up a secret laboratory. Now, that was not a DOD definition, but that was the way we saw it.

The matter was resolved by our not signing the contract. After some discussions with DOD we were willing to accept some of the limitations. Reluctantly we would have gone along with the requirement for prior clearance of foreign nationals working on the project. The others we could not accept.

The problem was that "sensitive" was going to refer to project elements that were to defined as the project went along. Most

141

would not be defined up front and some parts of the project would have been sensitive, some would not.

The resolution that seems to have been arrived at is a reasonable one. We need some test cases to see how it works. In the new policy, DOD will define projects as classified or not before the contracts are signed. The university has a nice clean decision. If it does not do classified work, it will not accept projects that have classified elements.

The DOD has further stated that work done at universities under its funding categories 6.1 and 6.2, will be considered fundamental and there will be no restrictions on open publications.

Occasionally the agency may wish to make a restriction and that will be put into the contract. Restrictions on publication and dissemination will not be applied on the basis of the "sensitive" classification proposed earlier in the year.

Part of the problem with the sensitive rating was that the areas to be protected included technologies that were seen to be militarily critical which I understand is 700 pages long and is classified. It is difficult to avoid transgressions when the excluded territory is unknown.

The real issue that seems to lie here is for the country to come to grips with what we need to limit to stem the flow of critical technologies to other nations. Is it the basic science, which is largely what is done in the universities; is it the products that eventually come out of that or is it the know-how in between the two? There have been several studies done that say it is the latter. It is the technological know-how that is critical.

An interesting point to me is that this country is faulted for not having been as agressive in the development of that know-how and the applications of it to our defense as have some other countries. In this particular case, Russia is seen as having done better than we have in the military technological development area. It is the same theme we have been singing with regard to basic research and industry. We have not had a tight enough coupling of research to development to undertake the next step after the basic recovery.

I am going to stop at this point. I am not sure the issue of sensititive research is resolved. Certainly it seems to be with DOD, but currently the laws that will control exports are being rewritten and it may be that we will still have a gray area involving technology transfer abroad in which we work out in individual cases how to control without compromising some of our basic values.

The Corson Report referred to a gray area and I think there may still be some residue of it left. Let me tell you of another event which occurred last Friday. A faculty member came in and said he had a problem with regard to sensitive research. I thought it did not exist any more, but this case came about in the following fashion.

He had been aproached by a corporation which had said that it would like him to undertake a research project with funding provided as a grant. It was to be a grant with "no strings attached", simply involving a check delivered to do work in an area.

The problem arose when the details of the proposed project were considered. It would be highly desirable for the work to be done using a software package which that corporation owns. Part of that software package is sensitive because it is listed on the militarily critical technologies list and, therefore, we are back in the same boat and we may have to turn down that particular project.

What would really be best is if we could discover in some fashion whether it really is a critical technology or not. That should be what should resolve this issue. As far as I know, we have no way of doing that. The issue, I suppose, is whether that list is the right list.

I have tried to give a few examples of how governmental policies, both state and federal impact a research university. Effects are felt whether or not the policies are directed toward the research effort and not all are supportive of governmental interests in stimulating industry-university collaboration.

Now I will stop and respond to questions.

DISCUSSION

DR. PFEIFFER: Heinz Pfeiffer, Pennsylvania Power and Light. I will take one place where I think there is not very good communication between industry and university and I would like to respond to that because it causes industry a great deal of trouble the other way.

That is, so often in the university, particularly in the renewable energy area, someone will calculate it takes 90 cents to build something including direct labor and materials and, therefore, should be available to the public for a dollar. Typically in industry the direct labor and material may be one-fourth or one-fifth of the cost.

When industry does not respond, very often the university will go public about our reluctance to accept these wonderful new things at economics the university figured out and it does cause industry difficulty.

DR. BARKER: I understand that. One of the points I would make in response is, it is not a university position usually you are dealing with. We are a land grant university and sometimes have to struggle with whether we are going to take a university or college position on an issue about which individual faculty members hold strong, and often opposing, views.

What you are dealing with, then, are generally individual faculty members who are taking their own position on an issue. While I recognize that this does not help a great deal, it just says they are not very good economists.

One of the things about universities is, of course, you can be an amateur at anything and to some degree get away with it.

DR. HERBERT: George Herbert, Research Triangle Institute. I think I also stand here as Chairman of the Board of Microelectronics Center of North Carolina. Not a question, but a comment with respect to state initiatives, an observation I think is quite important -- I realize with the number of university people here and the paucity of state government people I am really giving a sermon to the already ordained -- but because what is happening in North Carolina has been studied by nearly all of the contiguous states in the United States, it has given me an opportunity to see some of the other state programs and talk with people about them.

I think one of the tremendous, terrible mistakes made by state economic development planners or chamber of commerce type people is the mistake of believing that universities are simply a

144

resource that can be used without truly involving the universities in the total planning process.

I would use North Carolina as an example with respect to the Microelectronics Center of North Carolina.

Early in 1980 Governor Hunt had a dream, a desire, to try and make the state a center for that industry. But as he planned his program or rather as he attempted to establish his objectives, he did it in concert with Bill Friday, the president of the university system; Terry Sanford, the president of Duke; and the president of the community college system.

He did not come out with a goal until it had been developed with those people and then actually development of the plan for it was assigned to an assemblage of senior faculty members from the universities that were going to be involved.

As a result of that involvement, there is tremendous statewide belief and support, which has led to the appropriation since 1981 of 46 million dollars for that effort.

The involvement of the universities, rather than simply the use of the universities, I think has given a base of confidence that assures continuity of the program, in contrast to some of the others I have seen in other states.

So the sermon I always try to preach is you cannot just use universities, they must be involved in the planning process.

DR. BARKER: I would just add to that my experience in developing something on a smaller scale, although the budget is beginning to look in the 40 million dollar range by now. This was the biotechnology program we put together at Cornell. We started without thinking it would involve the state. It started as a campus initiative. We decided that there was a need for us to work more closely with industry and we currently have three corporations who are working with us.

The thrust of the program which we felt and the corporations bought on to was to pursue basic research, which we felt was what we were pretty good at, as the theme of the program. The corporations agreed with that because they saw that basic research in biotechnology really was what was going to matter ten years from now, not next year.

Interestingly, the state came into the picture afterward with an announcement it was going to identify centers for advanced technology. We felt we should apply since one of them was going to be in biotechnology in relation to agriculture and that sounded like a clear invitation.

The state, however, is much more concerned about the short-term activity. They are also more concerned, which I welcome, that we find wasys of working with smaller businesses.

The initiative for the program at the state actually came out of a council which had very few representatives from the university. Right now I see there is a bit of a struggle between the university and the centers program to come to grips with what is the best way for this thing to work. I would agree with you, in other words.

DR. WEBSTER: Barbara Webster, University of California at Davis. Mr. Barker, I wanted to comment on and elaborate on your reference to the matter of indirect costs/matching funds/cost sharing and another ramifications of the impact which this has on universities, or at least particularly on my own university.

The matching funds/cost sharing is widely regarded as a policy, but, in fact, it is a procedure which is followed by various federal agencies in which it is unevenly applied and often applied after the fact.

For example, although for the purchase of large pieces of equipment it is well-known that agencies require cost sharing or matching, it is not widely known that some divisions within an agency, such as NSF, decide after the fact; that is, after the grant is made, to impose a cost sharing or matching funds requirement on an individual grant.

This is done after the grant is made and it is applied unevenly. The University of California at Davis is widely regarded as well managed fiscally and so it is assumed, rightly or wrongly, by agencies such as NSF that we can scare up the money after the fact.

We are put in the position then of finding money for an individual awardee for matching funds on a piece of equipment after that grant is made, after it is approved by a peer review board and after it is awarded. This causes undue difficulty for us.

DR. BARKER: Amen.

DR. WEIGLE: I am Bob Weigle, Army Research Office. I guess we are the principal Army agency that deals with the university community. With respect to the classification issue, I just point out that none of the work that we support at the present time under contract with the university is of classified character.

146

However, I also represent the interests of a number of Army laboratories within the Army Material Command in the research end of the spectrum and I think there you have to recognize that they are closer to the application issue. In some instances I think some work of the university community may well turn out to be of a classified character. I am thinking in terms particularly of some of the work in the chemical biological defense area, for example.

The other thing that I point out is on the instrumentation grant, we also administer that for the Army, and, as you know, the DOD has made a commitment from each service of ten million a year for that purpose over the next two years to go beyond this current year.

One of the things that we found, you talked about matching kind of funds, was that we sort of felt that in some cases the universities really were not up front with us because we got promises of matching funds, but then we found out when we dig deeper, these funds were actually coming out of other government agencies.

I just point out that really does not serve the purpose of the universities in getting more money into the instrumentation area because you are going to get that kind of money from both agencies, government invested in any event. So really to try to solicit the support of the industry community or from university funds I think is to your advantage. So I just point that out. There is a desire on our part to see matching funds, but it does not really serve you if it is from the government.

DR. BARKER: Well, the only cases I know about in which that was being done there was already existing grant support from two agencies to a project or to a central serve-type instrumentation and, therefore, both agencies were approached at the same time. It has always been made very clear in the proposal that both agencies are being approached.

DR. WEIGLE: We have seen that, but we have seen other instances where it is kind of fuzzy about where the other matching funds were coming from and then we found that it really was out of NSF or one of the other agencies.

DR. BARKER: Well, one of the difficulties the university has in dealing with that is that if DOD, for example, puts out a request for instrumentation and puts a two-month deadline on when you can apply and then six months after that there is going to be a response, that gives the people at the universities maybe six months to find that other funding from some other agency.

If it is a significant chunk, industry generally cannot move

147

that quickly unless they already have a very tight relationship with the university. It is very difficult, in other words, to bring these rather large entities, government agency and industry, together and get them to support the same project.

DR. SPRIESTERSBACH: Spriestersbach, Iowa. Bob, there seems to be an assumption when we talk about information flow in the worldwide intellectual community that it primarily is a drain from the US to other parts of the world. I suppose some of us think that maybe there is a reciprocity. I simply do not know. There are some scientists, yourself included, here. I would be interested to hear what some folks' views were about whether there is a balance sheet that ends up sort of zero or whether it is a big negative on our part.

DR. BARKER: If you want to read something on that there is an article in the first issue of Issues in Science and Technology by Roland Schmitt dealing with it, and clearly dealing with it more from the point of view of industry, in which he asserts, and I tend to agree with this, that it is certainly a two-way street, that when visitors come they bring things with them and there is a lot of value to that.

If you look at how we have been staffing some of our industries and some of our universities in the last ten or 15 years, then people like me, who came from other places, have been a significant part of that staffing pattern. I would hate to see us lose that in any substantial way. I do not think anybody, however, is really trying to close the whole thing down. It is the Eastern European bloc that is a focus for concern.

DR. HANSEN: John Hansen, TRW. I represent a company that has considerable defense work, particularly classified activity, and I am involved in some of the interactions we have with universities.

A comment, I think you stated the problem very correctly and accurately Bob, about the security problem. But since I work one end of it, let me make a few comments on it.

Industry obviously is restricted by the conditions we have to live under as imposed by DOD when we get involved in the classified arena and we have the alternative of either losing the business or getting out of that business. So the boundaries we have to work in are rather strict.

However, I have found in particular problems it pays to investigate thoroughly that particular issue. When you start reading the fine print you can bring outside of the gray area a particular activity which might appear to be inside the gray area. So it really pays to explore possibilities here.

148

The closer one gets to an application of the technology the tougher it is to bring it out of the classified arena, but nevertheless, I have been involved in some of the things and it really does pay to work the problem very carefully and a lot of times we are fortunate in finding ways to arrive at a mutually satisfactory solution.

DR. BARKER: Do you have access to information that allows you to get involved in making that judgment, whether the matter should or should not be on the critical list? One of the problems that universities have, they have no access to that information. So they have to deal with the issue in the absence of critical information needed to do what you suggest.

DR. HANSEN: Yes, sir. The answer is yes because we are dealing with that DOD agency which made that rule or put that item on the critical list and when we talk to that individual we can separate the wheat from the chaff and find out what the sensitive areas are in many instances. In some cases, where there are several organizations involved in the technology, it becomes more difficult obviously to get a consensus this is not classified or this is classified.

There is an area that I have not heard addressed and that is the proprietary nature of things. Most companies that do a lot of research tend to put a proprietary stamp on their activities and this is not necessarily conducive to trying to establish a good relationship with the university.

Again this is an area that has to be worked, because just as a matter of policy one tends to put a proprietary stamp on something just to be sure that it is properly protected or that if something comes out of all this work that is beneficial to us, we have not legally left the door open somebody else can expand.

The problem is the universities like to publish, they do not like to keep the proprietary stamp on these things. It does create a barrier between us that perhaps more working on will help resolve, but it is there. You can not ignore it.

DR. BARKER: I think most universities that are in the research business would like to come up with the modern day equivalent of the Vitamin D patent, which was one of the big winners, or synthetic penicillin or something like that.

So it is not that the universities are not interested in that and I think recent changes in laws which allow universities to give exclusive license on patents has certainly enhanced the university's interest and the individual faculty member's interest, in pursuing patents. Most universities will allow the faculty member who is involved in an invention to make some financial gain from it if it is licensed. So there are inducements there to seek patents.

Where it becomes difficult is if a company wishes to come on to the campus and puruse research which is proprietary all the way through, not just that it might have a patentable outcome but to do proprietary work.

Some universities have arranged matters so they can do proprietary work. There is a very innovative program at RPI which is set up to do proprietary research and development. We could not do that at Cornell, partly because we are a land grant university and therefore, have a public responsibility, partly because of the secrecy.

DR. HANSEN: There are lots of ways to skin a cat and do not let the first one stop you from reaching the objective. You can usually get there if you try hard enough.

CHAPTER THIRTEEN
"Impacts on Universities: II"

Dr. William Risen, Jr.
Brown University

Introductory Remarks

DR. PHILLIPS: Our next speaker is Bill Risen, who is Professor of Chemistry at Brown University. His entire faculty career has been spent at Brown. He has also been Chairman of the Chemistry Department there and is currently Associate Director of the Materials Research Laboratory.

He does consulting with industry. He has two research grants, one from the federal government and one from a company. And he was educated at Georgetown University and received his doctorate at Purdue.

DR. WILLIAM RISEN, JR.

What I will do is to try to talk about how government policies affect university researchers who are in the direct laboratory setting; the front line troops, if you will. And it is a story that really needs to be told in two parts.

One is what university scientists deal with on a day to day basis, and the other is what university scientists think about the big picture items; the issues which are on such an incommensurate time scale and money scale that they do not really affect the way scientists work on a day to day basis, but that they do worry about.

Before I begin talking about some of these day-to-day kinds of issues, though, there is what I would call a "big picture" generalization that really has to be made. That is that the United States is spending a lot of money on science. And it is spending it in what has been and still is largely an unassailably honest, well-intended and successful way.

This is so important that if I had to just say one thing and sit down, that would be it. It is really, I think, the overriding fact and it needs to be said explicit and perhaps more often than we do.

But as good as the system is, it can be better. For all of us it might be useful to take a look at some of the kinds of changes and some of the kinds of individual problems that we have.

151

While I cannot speak for anybody but myself, I have discussed some of these matters with a number of my colleagues around the country. What I will say, therefore, will be my own view, but I think it probably is not very far from what is the majority view.

Let me start on the most local level and consider the kinds of things that we have to worry about on a day to day basis. Perhaps the best way to start is to ask what our day is like. It is a great sport.

We spend about 50 percent of our time teaching school and about ten percent of our time doing those things that are important to a university, whether it is advising students, developing curricula, or serving in roles that make a university have a collegial nature.

That leaves about 40 percent of our time for research. Now, of that 40 percent, about half of it is used up writing proposals, reports, doing administrative work, building the apparatus of cooperation and programs that are necessary to gain support, and trying to figure out where the money is.

Now, that means that our professors are spending something on the order of 20 percent of their time actually doing research. Now, even if I am off by 100 percent and the number is 40 percent, that is an extremely poor rate of resource utilization.

If the chief executive officer of any organization went to his board of directors and admitted that he was using his plant, his capital, his personnel or anything else at the 40 percent utilization level, the board would conclude they had a major management problem and they would get a new CEO.

We have a major management problem because that is the level of utilization of our key resource.

Well, what can be done about it? When we recognize that more and more professors are going to more and more sources for more and more grants of relatively smaller and smaller amounts over shorter and shorter durations; and it is to the point where professors have three to (in one case I know) -- twenty-five proposals pending; and to the point where some are writing renewal proposals before the initial grant period starts; and when we are at a time where professors sometimes do not know what year they are writing about when they are writing proposals, reports and interim reports at the same time, we just need to make some kind of a change.

Now, what I think we need to do is to have grants and contracts that are for larger amounts and longer periods of time.

152

Now, the real problem is not the total amount, I think. As I said before the total amount is not unreasonable. However, if the money were concentrated in ways that can save professors' time so they can do what they are there for, and if the time scale can be made commensurate with the research to be carried out, then I think we can have a much more efficient system.

I personally believe we have a very good example of the solution to the problem in the National Science Foundation sponsored Materials Research Laboratories. These are relatively large group effort grants in the area of material science. While they take a lot of time for the few people who are administering them, many other people are freed to do research with the sense of continuity of support.

These are not universally supported ideas; nonetheless, I think that this particular laboratory program is a reasonable model.

The second issue I was going to talk about in some detail has to do with overhead or indirect costs. Since Bob has talked about it and there have been comments on it, I will be very brief.

I think all of us understand that there are some legitimate and recognized indirect costs. The university has to heat the buildings, turn on the lights, count the money, take care of the animals, and do all the other things that are necessary (and maybe even pay a small part of the president's salary). Those are important to do.

On the other hand, I and my colleagues, including colleagues from other institutions, estimate that between 10 and 40 percent of the overhead, the indirect costs, goes to deal with the government in relatively unnecessary ways.

Whether it is to prove that we do, in fact, take care of the animals, or to figure out what in the world this new Office of Management and Budget A-21-A form we just got in the mail -- that is a two years ago problem -- means, or to apply again for permission to buy a piece of equipment for which the grant has already been made, or to recognize how to reorganize budgets to deal with the tax law that was passed last July, it all takes money, takes away from research, and diverts the time and attention of professors from what they are there to do.

To take one tiny current example, I estimate that about two times ten to the two university bureaucracies, and one times ten to the three senior administrators are spending part of this year figuring out what to do with approximately two times ten to the fourth grants and contracts in order to deal with a provision of

153

the tax law that was passed in July, which will net the government on the order of one times ten to the minus five of its tax receipts.

Now, this is being done by people who are there because this is the sort of thing that happens all the time. And their time is being paid for by the tax receipts. In fact, it will cost a great deal more in federal money to do it than will be collected.

Now, to the actual overhead rate in a university. The overhead rate in a university, by and large, ought to be approximately constant over time because most of the elements scale in the same way all the other cost elements in the society, which go into the direct costs scale. Thus, it ought to be approximately constant over time. It is not even close.

Now, if you want to estimate what the cost effect of all of this is, probably the best way to do it is first to take the current average indirect cost rate and subtract from it the average indirect cost rate applied in 1954 or, in fact, any other base year of your choice. Multiply that by the direct (or what in the jargon is called the MTDC, modified total direct) cost, of research. That product, the product, again, on the direct cost times the difference in the indirect cost times the difference in the indirect cost over those two periods of time, really ought to give you an idea of how much money the government and the universities collectively are wasting as a result of the way in which they interact with one another.

I do not know what the effect of all of this is on time and research. I think it is too difficult to calculate, but it is also too large to tolerate.

Now, one other question that was addressed earlier has to do with matching funds. I would like to put a slightly different twist on this and recognize that eliciting matching funds for instrumentation, in particular, represents a part of an effort on the part of the government agencies to deal with the fact that there simultaneously is an enormous, crying need and not enough money.

Despite the fact that a number of agencies -- NSF, DOD, and others -- were able to increase the amount of money for instrumentation significantly, there still was not enough. Therefore, typically, the balance was struck at somewhere between 25 and 50 percent matching funds. I do not know what the current number is, but the latest one I have heard at NSF is somewhere around 40 percent.

In any event, what has happened in order to use the federal money to leverage other money from universities, in order to buy

154

as much equipment as possible and make as much equipment available as possible in the universities, and to bring the attention of others, including private industy, to the problem, is to elicit matching funds. The whole approach, whether it is a policy articulated in the wording of either the appropriations or authorization laws or in committee discussions leading to those laws, or whether it is simply an implementation procedure of the agencies, the fact is that it started to stretch the funds.

Now, for a while it all worked this way. What the matching fund policy did was to increase the amount of money, increase the distribution of equipment and bring the attention of industry and others to the problem. But there have been some effects, and I think we ought to know what they are.

One of them is that university administrators have begun to figure out how expensive their science departments are.

Now, this is an era of academic retrenchment and in such an era that is deadly. What it really means is the cutbacks in the physics departments are going to be greater than the cutbacks in the humanities departments.

Another effect is that to avoid this staffing problem what is going to happen, and what is happening, is the professors have become private sector fund raisers. We may not be very good at it, but we sure know how to stir-around and try it.

So what we have is a situation in which professors, after getting a grant for a piece of equipment, find they need matching funds for it. Then they have to start all over and write proposals, spend more time, and incur more delays just to get a piece of equipment that has already been granted.

Now, as I said, there are good reasons for this and we recognize what those are, so it is an effort worth making. But, for every one of us acting as a sender there has to be a receiver at the other end. The receivers are companies and they are being deluged by matching fund requests. They have had to set up their own bureaucracies to deal with them.

Now, somehow or other you feel like a choreographer has put in one more step in this dance than you can do without tripping over your own feet. The effect, I am afraid, is to make the situation much more complicated than it really needs to be.

I do not have a solution to propose. I wish I did, because I think that virtually each of the individual steps we have taken to get where we are makes sense in itself. There are some ideal kinds of solutions, such as just getting more money. But, I am not sure that we need do much more than recognize what the problem is, for the companies to make considerable efforts, for the agencies to attempt to be as flexible as possible, for the time scales to be worked out in such a way as to be as helpful as possible, and for university administrators to begin to put at the disposal of the professors that part of the university community with which they have not been in contact. That is what euphemistically is called "development" on most campuses, and means alumni fund raising and other such operations. Professors really need to approach a different community than they are used to dealing with in order to get matching funds, and I think it will be increasingly important for them to do so.

Let me move on to a couple of the "big picture" issues before we are finished. I will mention a few of them. I may not mention the few that are your pet subjects or that would have been the selection of somebody else, but let me mention a few that many of us are thinking about and talking about. I will put my particular twist on them and no doubt this will elicit some responses.

One has to do with the support of academic engineering. Engineering support initatives include the establishment of a National Engineering Foundation, the National Science Foundation Engineering Support Initative, and other proposals.

Now, engineers and scientists are different, but they are not to be differentiated on the basis of who does the work well, who uses more fundamental principles, who is more productive, who is more careful, or who has any attribute that gets them to the right answer better than the other. They are to be differentiated, of course, by the questions they ask.

Now, engineers need to deal with important product or process objectives, either on the short or long run, and to do that engineering professors have to have extensive industrial contacts. They need them. They need them not only to know what the relevant questions are, what the practical problems and goals are, and how their research can be applied, what needs to be done, but as universities are now set up they need them because they have to get a significant part of their academic salary from external industrial contracts.

Now, if the force to do that is removed, if it is removed because the National Engineering Foundation or National Science Foundation engineering initiative pays for that academic year salary or pays for the salaries of students and technicians that are now being funded by external industrial contracts with engineering departments, what will happen is -- you can be sure this is true -- the engineers will simply pay less attention to industry.

Then, engineering departments will simply become less like engineering departments and more like the early 1960's phenomenon we call engineering science departments.

Now, while it is a good idea to fund engineering well, and indeed probably considerably better than it is now, it does not strike the scientific, and I think for that matter, large segments of the engineering community, as a good idea to go this route.

What it will do is take money away from science and make engineers less like engineers. I suspect there are some people who do not agree with that.

The second major issue I really should mention has to do with the increasing politicization of science. The burning issues at the moments have to do with the tendency to view construction of facilities, placement of computers, funding and location of big tickets, big physics facilites, for example, as if they are public works projects. This is not a new issue. The mission agencies have been dealing with it for a long time.

In the last 25 years, for example, it has meant that an electronics laboratory appeared in Cambridge, Massachusetts, when John Kennedy was President. NASA decided that Houston would be a great place to build a facility under Lyndon Johnson's guidance. An accelerator appeared in Michigan, and on and on.

It is not a new problem at all. Even the NSF is strongly affected. It has to worry about everything from sensation-seeking congressmen to distributing science education funding on a demographic map of the United States and, of course, it must contend with the National Engineering Initiative idea that I just mentioned.

You might ask what is wrong with all of this? Well, in moderation there is probably nothing wrong with it. In fact, it may be an excellent idea. Given two equal needs for a building, you might ask, why not put up the building where construction workers need work, where unemployment is high, and where economic development is most badly needed? The answer is there is nothing wrong with that.

On the other hand, once science is in the big leagues politically, as it was described earlier, it is in a league where there are not any forces of moderation. That is the problem. In moderation these political considerations are just fine, but once you get into a game in which there are no forces of moderation, it is not so fine any more.

So the questions to answer right now are, is this to become

the norm, and what is next? The answers, I believe, are yes and Health and Human Services. Yes, it will be the norm for money to be tainted relative to our traditional values. College administrators will moan; they will moan that the only problem with tainted money is that there taint enough of it.

It is going to be a war, folks; I am afraid that there will be such a war unless somebody stops it. I think that what will survive the war will be very different from what we know now. I think the result will be the destruction of the private state university system as we know it. It will be replaced by a de facto set of national universities.

If you want to be a survivor of this, either plan to be associated with a national university, or plan to put a stop to this nonsense.

The other answer, what is next, is Health and Human Services. The health related budget and the way it is spent, the effect it has on medical care costs, the effect it has on keeping physicians from practicing and decreasing competition among physicians, the effect it has of keeping medical professors from teaching, and the effect it has on financing community hospitals is a giant political target.

This budget will either come crashing down or come in for a soft landing. If concerned people want that to have a soft landing, some key aspect of Health and Human Services funding and financing has got to be changed. It should be changed clearly and firmly as a message.

I would suggest that the discontinuance of the RCDA, Research Career Development Awards, probably is the best way to do that. They are readily identifiable, they have virtually zero net value and they can be dealt with clearly and cleanly.

There may be some disagreement about what the net value of RCDA's is, but having administered a few of those and having studied the effects on a reasonable size population, I am not convinced of their value.

The third major concern that I can talk about has to do with the overall setting of funding priorities in the government, deciding what fields should be supported, to what degree support should be for basic as opposed to applied research, and so forth.

It is clear there is not enough time to go into that in great detail, but I would mention a little about the selection of fields to be funded. That selection tends to occur either as a result of some kind of external pressure, the pressure from various groups external to the government to "do something," about some problem, "do something" in some area, for example, "do something" about Japanese supercomputers, or as a result of a group of scientists advising on what would be good to study.

Now, these are perhaps the two best ways for the nation's scientific agenda to be set and I do not have a better idea, but there are some drawbacks and we need to look at them.

The pressure to "do something" is usually too late and it often leads to wasteful efforts. That surely was true of the nation's response to energy problems. It may prove wasteful also in the areas of so-called generic research, such as generic research on manufacturing technology, generic research on polymer processing, and generic research in a number of related areas.

The advice of scientists sitting down collectively, smoking their pipes, and saying wise things is not a whole lot better. While it is as farsighted as possible, when you look at the result what you often see is simply a future tense statement of what participants in the group are already doing.

What that often leads to is fields that have too many people and too few ideas. We need to recognize that effect. The classic case in chemistry is physical organic chemistry. Those of you who are familiar with the field will understand what the issue has been. The effect probably describes several current areas in the field of chemistry; specifically organometallic chemistry and organic synthesis. Everybody has his own pet list.

There is another side of the problem though. Important fields that do not yet have a critical academic mass, such as solid state inorganic chemistry and solid state inorganic synthesis, are badly neglected under this system.

Another important issue that I can mention just very briefly has to do with the demography of science. I can mention only one example by way of illustration. That is the national laboratories. I was going to say something about chemical engineering demography, but I will not have time.

We all recognize that many national laboratories, such as the Department of Energy funded national labs, have an aging population. The age distribution is wrong -- the demographics are not right. There are many ways of putting that. As articulated by the Packard Commission Report, they also have an unclear mission in the current societal environment for nuclear energy.

What this means, by and large, is that there is an institutional imperative to do a lot more work in an area where the society seems to be saying they do not want any more.

Now, in some ways, at least in terms of demography, the Agriculture Experimental Stations at all of the Land Grant schools, except MIT (where they are still out looking for the cow) and the military arsenal laboratories, have had the same sort of problem.

The Packard Commission looked at these types of institutions in detail and I will not repeat their findings, but it is useful to see what we can learn from the experience.

The primary characteristic many of these labs share is that they went through a very fast build-up. For the labs that I mentioned, especially the arsenals and the DOE funded laboratories, the primary reason for that was World War II, of course.

Sputnik was the reason for the build-up and the demography at NASA laboratories. And, social concern, as articulated in the late 1960's and early 1970's, was the reason at EPA. These also will not age very gracefully unless something is done about them soon.

EPA is, in my opinion, the biggest problem. Its laboratories grew very fast. They grew large and they grew with very uneven quality out of a very small slice of one scientific generation in the United States. Their current populations are going to go through the system very poorly, and we need to deal with that problem directly.

If you had heard the "working scientist" view from one of my colleagues, you might have heard a different set of concerns. They might include nuclear waste disposal, supercomputers, control of intellectual property, national security, funding distribution for defense relative to civilian needs and many, many more. And, of course, you might have even heard some quite different opinions.

What I have tried to do is to give you a few ideas about what working scientists are dealing with on a day to day basis. And I've mentioned a few other thoughts about issues that are too large for them to really deal with at that level, but nonetheless seem important to the health of science.

DISCUSSION

DR. STEVENSON: Jim Stevenson, Georgia Tech. One of the strengths, I guess, that has not been mentioned and the indirect costs that we all sort of put in some sort of disrepute is the fact that at Phoenix a number of years ago, at NCAR, we heard about the efforts of Colorado State and their creative financing.

We have taken advantage of that and went out a couple years ago with industrial development bonds in the amount of about 25 million dollars. These are story bonds that pledge research revenues in the future towards paying off those bonds for buildings or equipment or whatever.

It does again impact the indirect cost because indirect cost does take a jump, but if the magnitude of the bonds is not excessive that percentage jump is not that great. So it does provide a flexibility, I think, for universities to do some creative work in addressing the needs of researchers.

DR. RISEN: One of the things I did as Chairman of the Chemistry Department at Brown for the 1970's was to agitate for and finally get a new chemistry building. That was financed through a higher education taxfree bond in the State of Rhode Island, which needs to be paid back -- I am taking donations now -- and you are quite right.

What happened, of course, is that the extra charges associated with building has had a significant impact on the overhead rate. I think that it is about 1.8 percent for a period of a couple years and then, of course, as this whole program is recapitalized, that will disappear, but other things will appear to take its place.

I might mention that it is important for those of you who are interested in some of these issues to see what the risk side of this is as well.

Colorado State did use part of its creative financing to obtain a supercomputer and the supercomputer utilization at Colorado State has been a contentious one in comparison both to other supercomputer capabilities available within the government, particular one close by, and the supercomputer availability in other universities in the United States.

So it has not been an unmitigated success, but not because of the financing scheme so much as what they decided to finance.

DR. CHERNIK: Cedric Chernick, the Searle Scholars Program. In a way it is a follow-up on what the previous individual pointed

161

out. It is almost naive to expect that the rate of indirect costs would increase at the same rate as the other components because of the building, because of the fact that fuel costs have gone up considerably faster than other costs and there are many contributing factors, which unfortunately are not increasing at the same rate as the other costs in the indirect cost rate.

I would also like to comment that I am in a grant making program and I think there must be two different ways of measuring the amounts of time the faculties spend in teaching because I have never seen anybody say they are approaching anything like 50 percent of their time in teaching. And finally I think that one of the problems --

DR. RISEN: Excuse me, can I interrupt. You are looking at one right now because if I were in Providence today right now I would be about ten minutes into a freshman chemistry lecture, which would be over at 11:00. I would have a chemistry 3 staff meeting from twelve to one and teach the laboratory from one to four today. Today would be completely gone.

Tomorrow there would be a couple of hours of office hours. This would be Monday, Wednesday and Friday. And that, together with the preparation, adds up to 50 percent of any reasonable construction of working hours.

I think it is probably true that it varies all over the lot and if we are talking about an assistant professor of philosophy who is teaching four courses a year, it is more. If we are talking about a medical professor, it probably needs to be investigated under a microscope.

But if we are talking about the average professor, I think that the total commitment of time and effort probably amounts to 50 percent of what you would construct as a reasonable workload.

DR. CHERNICK: I can give you a list of institutions where you might have a lower working load, if you'd like to consider some of them.

The final thing I wanted to comment on was the question of the larger grants. There is another side to that coin. There are a number of people out there who like to have the shotgun approach with the possibility if one institution turns them down, another one would accept them because the logical extension of what you say is to have all applications sent into one agency where there is one peer review group instead of spending the time of faculty sitting on peer review groups for a series of different agencies.

That peer review group would look at the application, would given it a rating, would send that rating out to the different federal agencies, and based on that one rating, they could make a decision whether or not they were going to fund it.

But I think you would find that most faculty would be a little apprehensive about one peer review group.

DR. RISEN: May I respond to that. Indeed the diversity of system is extremely important. It is important for a lot of reasons. It is important for justification of the funding in the first place, for the general sociology of the field in another.

On the other hand, we should be very careful to understand what really happens. What really happens is people spend a lot of time running around trying to find where the money is and how to get it. In the federal government probably about ten percent of the money that is spent on research and development is actually peer-reviewed. For the expenditure of funds within the United States overall my estimate is it is between three and four percent. For the other 96 to 90 percent of the money, the financial decisions about supporting research and development in the United States are not made on the basis of peer review.

Peer review is an extraordinarily powerful political shorthand for the sociology of a field. It is important that we have both the diversity of agencies and an understanding that peer review is an unassailable vehicle for making sure that those who actually understand the scientific problems have a say in what is good research to do. And I agree with that.

I agree with that entirely and what you are saying is precisely right, that the working scientist does have much greater confidence in the system because of it diversity.

DR. LEVINSON: Nanette Levinson, The American University, a unversity which some call a national university. I would like to expand on and perhaps provide a slightly different perspective on Cedric's and your comments on resource utilization.

While I agree very strongly with your call for larger contracts and grants and mechanisms that will provide more continuity in the contracts and grants, I take issue with your resource utilization arguments.

I think the comments Cedric just made and your reply illustrate, in fact, that there are very different percentages, differing not only by type of university and by field, but I think really with individual professors and researchers within any given university.

I think there is a more basic issue here. It is extremely difficult to break down teaching and reasearch into percentages.

163

I would argue for many faculties there really is a synergy between teaching, research and advising. It is very artificial to use a percentage argument.

Rather I wonder if it would not be better for us in universities to make the argument, in fact, that we need mechanisms for longer-term research contracts and larger research contracts and grants because of the quality of the work and also because of the nature of the research enterprise in each one of our disciplinary areas.

DR. RISEN: Yes, I think it is true there is a considerable synergy. And it is certainly true that every individual has a style of teaching and research that leads to different percentages, if, indeed, percentage distributions make sense.

I think, that, it is important to understand that very often on an hour by hour, day to day, week to week, month to month basis, professors have to decide what they can afford to do: can I or can I not afford to work on freshman chemistry laboratory experiment design; or can I or can I not afford to work on such and such a problem that has to do with interacting with people in the physics department and the engineering department in order to build a program, even though I know what this will do is take me away from doing some other parts of my job.

They are synergistic intellectually and they do feed on one another and reinforce one another, but there are still time and effort choices to be made. And, when those are made the roles look pretty separate.

DR. FREDERICK: Bill Frederick from Pennsylvania Power and Light Company. I would just like to make an observation here that I have or a feeling that I get. I hear most people say that those who provide the money are requiring more and more accountability and that is a problem, the overhead costs are getting higher and higher as a result of it and that those people who supply the money, specifically government and so forth, have the politicians controlling it that are very short-sighted. In other words, they are looking ahead just to the next election.

Now, I think that we should gain something from this in the sense that in this meeting there may be only ten percent of industry here, but the government engine which has the shortsightedness or short cycle of maybe each election is not quite true in industry and the way you can get money out of industry is to sell the product.

Now, I am not saying sell a specific research project. I am saying take what is already done and put more emphasis on the transfer of technology and when you get that communication with

164

industry that you have something that is worthwhile to them that you have done in the past, they are going to get their input in the front end of that engine. You will find the communication you develop is going to pay off in the end.

Therefore, I would propose that between now and the next meeting that we in NCAR make a strong effort to get more industry people involved in next year's meeting and the following meetings as a means of saying they are the ones that will provide the fuel for your scientific engine in the long term in the future.

DR. RISEN: Right. I think those comments are important and they come together in one particular issue that I did not have a chance to talk about. That has to do with the research and development tax credit, because that is, by and large, the expenditure of tax money.

If the question is accountability, then the question of tax expenditures through the R&D tax credit really comes down to a question of whether the government or the companies can spend taxes better. And that is really the ultimate accountability question in research and development expenditures by the country.

I think that in the absence of any other information, the nature of our democracy calls for the government to make those expenditures. That means that if industry is going to make those expenditures it has the burden of proving that it can do it better than the government. Perhaps making the time scale and financing scale commensurate will be precisely what industry can do that the government cannot.

CHAPTER FOURTEEN
"Impacts on Universities: III"

Donald M. Langenberg
University of Illinois at Chicago

Introductory Remarks

DR. PHILLIPS: We have heard from the provost and the faculty member, past and department chair, and it has now come up to the chancellor's level and we will get the view from that perspective of the impact of federal policies on universities.

Don Langenberg, as many of you know, has been a professor of physics at the University of Pennsylvania, also their Vice Provost for Graduate Education and Research, also there, too, involved as Director of their Materials Lab, Deputy Director of the National Science Foundation, and I think somewhere in there was interwoven some periods of Acting Director, and for the last couple of years has been Chancellor at the University of Illinois at Chicago. We look forward to Don's comments.

DONALD LANGENBERG

In considering what might be the impacts on universities of new Federal policies for R&D, it seems appropriate to begin by reviewing just what these new Federal policies might be. In the first session of this conference we heard Jim Ling of the Office of Science and Technology Policy describe this Administration's policies.

Jim began by stating two fundamental Administration goals. The first is a revitalized economy; as the economy improves, this goal is shifting toward maintenance of growth and improvement of our competitive position in the world economy. The second goal is a strong defense posutre.

Jim then stated three criteria which must be satisfied by Federally-supported R&D. The first is excellence. The second is relevance. (If I remember correctly, this used to be called "pertinence" in the early days of this Administration. I'm a little sorry to see us revert to this earlier and somewhat tarnished term.) By way of explanation here, Jim noted that a program can be considered relevant if it produces talented scientists and engineers or if it produces results which meet national needs.

The third criterion is appropriateness. A program is

appropriate if it falls within an area of Federal responsibility. Examples are programs which meet specific Federal needs in an area of exclusive Federal responsibility, e.g., defense, or programs which meet national needs in areas where the Federal government shares responsibility with other sectors. The latter include activities which contribute to improvement of the economy or to quality of life but which cannot be justified as the sole responsibility of one or more non-governmental sectors. Jim's example here was basic research. The Federal government does not bear the sole responsibility for the support or performance of basic research, but it is clearly the view of this Administration that the Federal government must share responsibility for basic research with other sectors.

Jim went on to assert that basic research is a good thing for three reasons: First, it produces science and engineering talent and is therefore presumably relevant. Second, it pushes forward our intellectural frontiers and provides new knowledge which is useful in our struggle to reach our national economic and security goals. Third, it stimulates productive partnerships among sectors.

I am led to several observations about these elements of Federal R&D policy, as described by an official Administration spokesman. First, they seem to me to be simple, concise, and reasonably clear. These are desirable characteristics of any policy. Whether one accepts and/or agrees with this policy or not, it does, it seems to me, provide a rational basis for judging and debating the merits of R&D programs.

Second, in the general form in which I have just recounted it, this Administration policy does not appear to be particularly new. With a few semantic changes, I believe it could be translated into policy statements by administrations of both parties over the past several decades. I do not mean to suggest that this lack of novelty is bad. Quite the contrary; I think it reflects an underlying basic bipartisan consistency in R&D policy which should encourage us all.

But, you will protest, we have long been buffeted by the shifting winds of Federal R&D policy. On a microscopic level that is probably true. Think how dull all our lives would be if they were not occasionally interrupted by news of the latest Federal outrage. I submit, however, that, macroscopically, Federal R&D policy has been remarkably stable and consistent since the fifties. While there have been shifts of emphasis and style, the overall Federal commitment to support of R&D has been reflected in almost monotonically increasing Federal obligations for R&D funding for more than three decades. The balance among institutional performers of R&D has shifted and will continue to do so, but slowly. A glance at the scientific journals over the years shows much the same institutions represented, with perhpas a few waxing or waning in influence.

Fundamentally, then, Federal R&D policy has for some time been stable and consistent and, I believe, is likely to continue to be so. Against this underlying stability, however, must be placed changing interpretations of the policy, changing notions of what is meant by "excellence", "relevance", and "appropriateness." These may not warrant the label "new policies", but they and the response of the multi-sector national R&D enterprise to them do portend evolutionary changes which bear watching. Let me discuss in a little more detail two current examples.

The first is commonly labeled "science and engineering education." In the early days of the present Administration, influential Administration leaders held the view that Federal involvement in education was inappropriate and that education was the responsibility of state and local governments and the private sector. This interpretation of the term "appropriateness" led to the conclusions that the Department of Education ought to be abolished and that the National Science Foundation budget for science and egnineering ought to be identically zero. Meanwhile, however, the growing national concern about our ability to achieve the Administration's primary goals of economic vitality and military security has led to a broader understanding of the relationship between that ability and the state of our technology. This in turn has highlighted the need for scientists and engineers who can create technology and for citizens who can use it. It is but a short further step to recognition of the importance of a strong educational system, an importance underscored by a host of recent studies and reports. As a result, we have seen a flowering of interest in education in general, and science and engineering education in particular, of a sort we have not had since the post-Sputnik period. State and local governments are reexamining their responsibilities for and their investments in education. The private sector is assuming a more active role, in its own and the national interest. And the Congress and the Administration are reasserting and redefining an appropriate Federal role in the nation's educational system. The Department of Education has not been abolished, and the National Science Foundation has been provided with more money for science and engineering education than it can just now comfortably spend. Jim Ling several times mentioned the production of science and engineering talent, as a test for relevance and as one of the reasons why the Administration feels basic research needs to be supported.

Here we have an element of Federal R&D policy of great importance to our research universities. It is these institutions which develop and foster the science and engineering talent upon which our technological future depends, particularly at the graduate level where training takes place in close association with the performance of research. Our universities have long been committed to the joint production of new knowledge through research and of trained manpower. The existence of a Federal policy which is supportive of that commitment is both encouraging and of enormous importance.

Equally encouraging and important is the resurgence of interest in education, including science and engineering education, on the part of state and local governments and the private sector. In his 1983 Ferguson Lecture at Washington University, George Pake, Group Vice President of the Xerox Corporation, said: "Inventions of ultimate technological and economic significance once could be made by intelligent, persistent thinkers with little formal higher education. Edison, the Wright brothers, and Henry Ford come to mind. Modern technological advance is a different story. Consider the transistor, the laser, or synthetic insulin ... You don't find these associated with tinkering in a basement or a garage ... Thus, the modern R&D enterprise is inextricably linked with the research university, which draws its graduate students from the colleges. There is a great big E that comes before R&D; I shall refer to the E,R&D macrosystem."

I heartily agree with George, and I am delighted to learn that the present Administration is coming round to his view. I think it is terribly important that the private sector and state and local governments, as well as the Federal government, meet their responsibilities in education. And I believe that all of us restrict our concern for the E to graduate education in the sciences in education only at great peril, for the E system itself is a strongly interdependent one and needs to be considered in its totality from top to bottom, from K through 12 and from the freshman year through the Ph.D.

Let me turn now to what I consider a second major feature of this Administration's R&D policy. Jim Ling noted that "appropriateness" covers cases where the Federal government shares responsibility with other sectors. He also gave as one of the reasons for Federal support of basic research that it stimulates productive partnerships among sectors of the R&D community. As I see it, this element of the Administration's policy is intended to encourage the further development of a strongly-interacting E,R&D system, one in which all the sectors represented at this NCAR conference combine in synergistic ways to yield better results faster. These might include various sorts of industry-university relationships, and interconnections between universities, the national laboratories, and venture capitalists. Such relationships have of course been the subject of considerable attention in recent years. There are many factors other than Federal policy which are driving the sectors of the E,R&D system toward stronger interactions, but the existence of such a Federal policy is, I think, of major significance.

I am reminded of certain phenomena which occur in physical systems studied by my fellow condensed-matter physicists. These are collective phenomena which occur when large numbers of simple particles interact strongly and which cannot be understood or predicted simply by adding up the behavior of individual more-or-less independent particles. When we seek to create new types of interactions among the several sectors of the national R&D enterprise, I think we are all really hoping that something new will happen, something that would not happen if we all just went our own ways independently. I think there are real reasons to believe that that hope will be fulfilled, and I applaud the Administration for articulating encouragement of productive partnerships as an element of its R&D policy.

There is another feature of strongly-interacting physical systems which, in the present analogy, may give us pause. In such a system, the behavior of each participating particle is strongly perturbed by its interaction with the others. Now universities perhaps more than other institutions have depended on the free and relatively unfettered functioning of individuals, their faculty members, operating under the guiding principles of academic freedom. As institutions, universities have sought to maintain the maximum possible independence from certain types of external influence. Many of us believe that this feature of academe is of fundamental importance to the effectiveness of academic institutions. As we explore the benefits to our universities and to the nation of enhanced interactions with other sectors of the R&D enterprise, we must be very careful not to perturb unduly certain fundamental aspects of the academic environment. I think I need not tell you that many university faculty members consider this issue to be among the most important ones our universities face today. Nor is this an issue of importance only to universities and their faculties. Where there is shared effort in search of mutual benefit, there is also shared risk and the potential of mutual loss.

As I applaud the current thrust toward productive partnerships among R&D sectors and caution about possible negative aspects of such partnerships, I wish I were also able to predict where our current efforts will lead. Unfortunately, I cannot. I can say, with considerable confidence, that, whatever the impacts of Federal policy and intersector activity in this area may turn out to be for universities, they will be substantial. Whether they are good or bad will depend on how we all address the relevant issues in the coming months and years.

Let me give an example of a Federal initiative which I believe is having and will have unintended and, in this case, positive impacts on the university research community. Earlier in this conference, Milton Stewart discussed the role of small businesses in the R&D enterprise. He noted a tendency to think of university-industry relationships primarily in terms of large industries, to the chagrin of small businesses, and characterized the attitude of small businesses toward universities as often antagonistic and hostile. He pointed to the R&D programs mandated by the Small Business Innovation Development Act of 1982 as by far the best of Federal programs for small business.

During my time at NSF, I saw evidence for all of Milt's points. On one occasion I testified before a Congressional committee in support of the Small Business Innovation Development Act, on behalf of NSF and the Administration. As most of you know, the research universities by and large strongly opposed that legislation, on the grounds that legislated set-asides for any class of R&D performer are a poor way to do business, and that the set-aside funds would inevitably come out of the hides of the research universities. I remember having personal reservations of the same kind. I have since come to believe that the Small Business Innovation Development Act may well turn out to be one of the most valuable recent acts of our government on behalf of R&D, in all sectors including the universities.

The anticipated negative effect of the Act for the research universities, a reduction in available R&D funding, may or may not be real; I suspect it will be forever indeterminate. I believe, however, that we are beginning to see some very real positive effects. Fully half of the grants made by NSF under its prototype Small Business Innovation Research program have involved significant participation by university faculty members with the small business grantees. I am aware of several examples on or near my own campus of faculty with major roles in SBIR grants from other agencies. The potential benefit here, both for the small business concerned and for the faculty member's university, is tighter coupling between the university, its faculty, and a business of a type which spawns much of the technology of the future and with which we in the universities have not in fact thought much about interacting. I believe this will have both direct and indirect benefits for all concerned, in the long run. While familiarity sometimes breeds contempt, it also often breeds respect. If we can lessen the misunderstanding and occasional hostility which seems to exist between the small business community and our universities, I think we can take a big step toward creating mutually supportive relationships with implications extending far beyond our immediate R&D needs.

I'd like now to make a couple of general points about R&D policies. As we work to shape policies for our increasingly complex and strongly-interacting E,R&D system, I think we have

171

and will continue to have an awful problem with incommensurate characteristic time scales. One occasionally hears this mentioned, but I don't think we have ever really confronted this. You will recall that one of the questions asked of Jim Ling earlier was whether the Administration was satisfied that its new policies are having the desired effects. In this, the last year of this Administration's first term, that is a reasonable question to ask. Jim's answer was of course an upbeat on, but I think the real answer is that it is far too early to tell, that the ultimate effects of the policies of this Administration will not be fully understood until after Mr. Reagan has left office, whether he serves one term or two terms. In this, I don't think the relevant time scale differs much from the time scale on which one begins to know whether a particular scientific development has led to a viable technology, surely a matter of a decade or more in most cases.

We in the universities also tend to think in terms of long time scales, in cycles of student generations, four years or maybe ten if one considers graduate or professional programs. And for those in universities or those who seek to understand them, it is important to remember that there is an even longer underlying time scale for universities. I need not look very far to find an example. Nearby is the College of William and Mary, established in 1693 "for the purpose of Indian instruction." Since that date our country has undergone three or four major transformations in the structure of its government. The last gentleman to occupy the Governor's Palace here in Williamsburg has long since packed his bags and gone back to England, taking with him the Crown's authority over the Commonwealth of Virginia. The Confederate States of America have come and gone. The College of William and Mary remains. True, it has grown and adapted itself to changing circumstances. Its student body no longer is composed solely of Indians. It is currently playing a major role in an effort to build an electron accelerator to study nuclear matter, a function its founders could hardly have forseen. But William and Mary retains the fundamental functions of any academic institution and displays the longevity which seems to be characteristic of such institutions. I suspect that no industry represented at this conference is half so old as William and Mary. Absent a nuclear war, in another three hundred years I would expect these industries either to have died or transmuted themselves into something quite unrecognizable in present terms. William and Mary will still be here.

My point is that universities are, with very few exceptions, man's most durable, stable, and adaptable institutions. This fact strongly conditions the kind of thinking a university must do when it confronts a Federal policy change and considers its implications for the research and education environment tomorrow. We must think not only in terms of the lifetime of a generation

172

of students or a generation of faculty, but of the viability and vitality of the institution in the next century and beyond.

It seems to be difficult in a society devoted to instant gratification and the quarterly financial report to refrain from asking the kind of question Bob Barker reported he had had from a New York official: "Dr. Barker, what sort of indicators can you provide us which will tell us six months hence whether today's R&D investment has begun to achieve the desired results?" But we ought to try and, if we can't resist, we ought to keep in mind the time scales on which policies come to fruition, scientific breakthroughs become taken-for-granted technologies, and universities live. Patience and the long view should not be virtues practiced only by the Chinese.

My other general point about R&D policies is related to John Holmfeld's presentation earlier in this conference. John told us that we may be at a watershed in national science policy. He mentioned several major science policy studies, including one being undertaken by the House Science and Technology Committee. I just want to go on record saying that from my point of view, it is difficult to think of any Federal policy which is not a science policy or an R&D policy. Sometimes the effects on R&D of a Federal policy are indirect, second or third order, or unintended, but they're almost always there and often they're signficant. Let me mention a few examples.

Tax policy is, either directly or indirectly, R&D policy. It has general economic effects which affect the climate for support and performance of R&D. It usually implies specific tax provisions which determine levels of private sector support for universities or the ability of business to invest in R&D.

The list of national issues with high emotional content which includes abortion has a recent addition, "animal rights". Several universities, including the University of Pennsylvania, have already been drawn into controversy on this issue, and I forsee serious Federal policy questions in this area. The importance of animal models in biomedical research makes this an R&D policy issue.

Any policy concerning provision of or reimbursement for health care is perforce an R&D policy, because it inevitably strongly affects the functional and financial viability of the largest research laboratory on many university campuses, the university hospital.

Some aspects of foreign policy or trade policy are also certainly R&D policy, for they affect the flow of scientific and engineering personnel and information across international boundaries. The issue of scientific communication and national

173

security has been an active one in recent years and I expect it to remain so.

To repeat my point, I can think of no Federal policy which has no implications for the nation's R&D enterprise and which, therefore, is not an R&D policy, at least in part. This may be just another indication that R&D has "hit the big time" and become a major element of the national political arena.

I'd like to conclude by returning to an issue mentioned earlier in this conference, one which will provide an interesting example of the application of this Administration's R&D policies. This is the issue of university research facilities.

There is growing evidence that the research universities of our nation have a serious problem with their physical facilities, particularly their research laboratories. In some ways this problems parallels the universities' research instrumentation problem, which surfaced earlier and which has induced substantial responses from both the Federal government and the universities. The facilities problem appears to be equally real and perhaps of greater magnitude; one hears reports of needs for hundreds of millions of dollars in single institutions and of price tags running into many billions for the total national research universitiy community. The situation in my own institution, the University of Illinois, is illustrative. The two campuses of the University in Chicago and in Urbana/Champaign have a combined physical plant with a replacement value on the order of two billion dollars. Reasonable estimates would suggest a need for a continuing investment of something like 50 to 100 million dollars each year, just to keep that plant in good working condition and to adapt it to the changing needs of the University. In recent years the State of Illinois has been able to provide only a small fraction of that amount for renovation and rehabilitation. We thus have a very substantial deferred maintenance problem. It is serious enough for general purpose facilities like classrooms, but it is particularly bad in research laboratories, which must serve today's research needs, not those of half a century ago. This leads to some extremely awkward circumstances; it is galling, I assure you, to face the necessity of rejecting half a million dollars in industry support for research, not because faculty and student talent is lacking, but because there's no place to do the research.

Who's problem is this? Is it the universities' and their public and private patrons'? Is it the Federal government's? We have here an interesting case in the application of the "appropriateness" element of the Administration's R&D policy, coupled with the aspects of that policy which are pushing us toward a more strongly interactive E,R&D system with its implied shared responsibility. To me these mean that it's everybody's

174

problem, that each sector needs to address the problem according to its own lights. Exactly what this means will be, I believe, a very important topic for discussion during the next several years.

I would note that, for the Federal government, this issue has already asserted itself in the guise of "pork barrel science politics." Many universities, driven by their desperate needs for new research facilities, have abandoned the traditional Federal R&D funding channels and adopted methods more commonly used to fund river and harbor projects. This has aroused deep concerns in the university research community about erosion of the peer review process. These concerns are serious and will not easily be allayed. The urgent need to do so is another reason to seek an intersectoral understanding of how we are going to address the university research facilities problem.

I have tried here to suggest some ways in which Federal policies for R&D affect universities and to raise some of the issues which all of us will be addressing in the next several years in the context of current policies. Though these current policies reflect substantial underlying stability and consistency over several decades, their implementation depends on their interpretation, and this can and does change more rapidly. This, together with the fact that the issues, or at least our view of them, also change will surely provide plenty of meaty material for NCAR conferences for many years to come. I look forward to joining you in the debate.

DISCUSSION

DR. HILL: I am Chris Hill with the Congressional Research Service. I have seven or eight questions. I will try to limit myself to two.

First, if we continue your sort of mechanical analogy of the R&D system, it seems to me it has another attribute I would like to have your response to.

That is that it amplifies any small perturbation, it is rather an underdampening system. Therefore, while we may see the policy environment as being relatively stable and relatively monotonic, in fact, the little perturbations make a great difference.

A piece of evidence would be the fact that the Engineering Research Centers Programs, which offers only ten million dollars, which is 1/100ths of one percent of the nation's R&D spending for next year has led to the generation of 160 proposals which must have involved 1500 people, hundreds of firms, etc. So the resources are large and they are the best resources in those universities, most of which went to an internal competition even to get that far. So there's an enormous amplification of any external disturbance.

Second point, I wanted to ask was about your focus on the appropriateness criterion which Jim did lay out quite clearly. Those essentially economic arguments were developed 25 years ago to provide a rationale for a federal role in R&D. They were to open the door. They did not tell us how far the door would be opened. The appropriateness argument is essentially an unquantified argument about what the federal role might be.

What may be different in this administration is the use of an inappropriateness argument. Rather than seeing the arguments about risk and externality as opening the door to federal role, they have been applied asymmetrically to say if we cannot find a good reason then we ought not be there and that uses the same argument not to open. But delimit and that is a very different use, which leads to the kind of problems you may have encountered.

DR. LANGENBERG: I am going to assume all these questions are addressed to the whole panel and if there is a tough one I am going to direct it to Bill or Bob.

The mechanical analogy, as you call it, is an interesting one because you can take it a long way if you really want to push it. Amplification and underdampening are terms applicable to linear systems. This is a highly nonlinear system.

176

One of the things that brought that model to mind was some recreational reading of a couple of papers by John Hopfield about theoretical simulation of how the brain and certain computer systems store memory.

It is evidently now becoming increasingly clear that the human brain does not store a memory as one might have supposed twenty years ago, information bit by bit in single neurons. The information is stored collectively across huge masses of strongly interconnected neurons; memory is probably a state of large collections of strongly interacting neurons.

There are all sorts of fascinating things going on in such systems that I think may well be characteristic of the system we all live and work in. I think we have to be a little careful about using linear systems to describe what we are trying to do here.

With respect to the second comment, yes, you are absolutely right. This administration has taken the view that if you cannot show it is appropriate, you should not do it.

I think what the administration is saying in the policy statement that Jim Ling presented, and this has not changed much since 1981, is that we are defining certain things as appropriate.

One of those things is basic research and that opens the door for support of basic research, and I would submit, opens the door not only to direct support of basic research in single-principal-investigator projects, but for support of all aspects of the system that produces basic research, including facilities.

DR. BAEDER: Don Baeder, Occidental Petroleum. I would like to make two comments. First, your opening statement where you quoted the president of some company as saying large industries do not happen in garages any more. I think we are looking at a personal computer industry that now approaches multi billions that did start in a garage.

The second one I will give you, CAD/CAM, which started in many professors' offices on software programs. The biogenetics revolution started in many small places. So I really do not believe the era of the garage or the small laboratory is by any means behind us and we have a dream of large systems.

The second comments I would like to make to the whole panel is on the area of university-industrial relations. It is my opinion that if you are trying to build this relationship on science and technology only as the common denominator between the two, it is like pushing a wet noodle through a sieve. You cannot do it.

On the other hand, if you just look around, where there was some relevance on the part of the university, industry is there. Where there is relevance to meeting human needs on the part of the university you are going to find industry is there trying to work cooperatively with them.

I am very familiar with one experience which I will call the Carnegie-Mellon University Experience and it is a private university.

We had a new president about nine years ago who decided he had graduated the last student whose parents were going to come to him and say, look, I spend all this money and my kid cannot get a job. He spent three years in graduate school and two years in a postdoc and got a beautiful degree in physical organic chemistry and cannot get a job anywhere.

So he said we are not going to do that. We are going to decide what are some very relevant areas and we are going to concentrate on these and build on them and we are going to turn out people who are trained to go into the profession or the university and teaching, one of the two.

Now, I show you some things that he did, if you will just allow me. First of all, he decided that robotics was going to become a very important area and good robotics required sensors and they were on the forefront of laser and other research in sensors. So he formed a robotics institute. It has a lot of money.

In fact, they come to companies and say, look, we want to work with you. They came to one of our companies, Iowa Beef. And if you do not think the slaughtering of the thousands of animals that goes on every day is not something that can be automated, they thought sensing because each animal is different. And they said we have money, we want to work with you. And there is work going on.

Westinghouse funded a major program there in robotics with them. So where they begin to get relevant, the industry is there.

He also decided every student was going to have a computer. That is very fashionable, but he added on this that each of those computers were going to talk to each other and talk to the central unit and when a student leaves he will take his computer with him and he will be able to talk to this system.

178

He had two major companies bidding against each other to get into a cooperative program with them and they picked IBM. Thirty million dollars IBM is spending there in the next three or four years to do this.

I could go on about things he has done. His business school, he now believes the business area is going to be regulatory, heavily regulatory oriented, and brought in a new head of the business school from the FAA who led the deregulation of the airlines industry.

All I am trying to say is that there is a role for the university president, for the deans of science and engineering to begin to think about their university as an important area that is producing students and producing technology relevant to the needs of science. And I tell you if you do this, you are going to have great university-industry-government relations.

DR. LANGENBERG: Two comments, and perhaps then I could turn to the rest of the panel: George Pake did not say, and I was trying not to say, that new industries, high tech industries in particular, no longer start in garages. They do, or they start in somebody's incubator facility or elsewhere.

What George was saying is they are no longer founded in garages by people who dropped out of high school, as they sometimes were in the 19th century. They are being founded by people with bachelor's degrees in engineering from the University of Illinois or by Ph.D.'s from Carnegie-Mellon or wherever.

The second comment I wanted to make is that you are absolutely right about presidents and deans and the like. You should understand, however, that there is a good deal of ingrained suspicion within universities among many faculty about presidents and deans who talk like that. I can give you chapter and verse from personal experience.

DR. BAEDER: I do not want to tell you there is not a lot of suspicion there and there were for a number of years. When he said we are not going to be everything to everybody, we are going to focus our faculties in areas, the first question came up was what about tenure?

He said we will honor tenure, but if the tenured professors want to stay with us in areas that we are not trying to be the top in, we will keep them but, he said, they would not stay, if they are any good they will go to another university that is really focusing in their area. And that is exactly what happened. He had no tenure problem.

DR. CHERNICK: Cedric Chernick. I think I have friends here

179

from the academic community. I may not have after I ask this question. It is directed at Don and all I can say is forewarned is forearmed.

The federal government made a decision a long time ago that it had some responsibility towards the building problem and it allowed in A-21 for recovery of building depreciation costs. I would like to know what the rationale is for the government to pay again for money that it has already paid and the universities have chosen to use for a different purpose?

DR. LANGENBERG: That is a tough one and Bob has volunteered to take it.

DR. BARKER: The world I have been living in has experienced considerable inflation. Building use allowance is two percent a year on the cost of construction not the current value of buildings. I think, therefore, if you expect the university to use a two percent use allowance to construct the facilities needed now it is never going to happen.

DR. CHERNICK: I am still looking for examples where any institution has set any part of that money aside and has used it, even if it is only for building --

DR. BARKER: I can point to the example of Michigan State, which built a building and was told it was in violation of the law for doing it.

DR. LANGENBERG: He has answered it better than I could. Cedric, you are still my friend.

DR. BEHRENS: I have a question, but I think it is also a comment. The engineering and science disciplines several times over this conference have taken great pride in achieving the major leads in policy focus for the federal government and I think that recognition is clearly deserved, it is needed. At 50 billion dollars per year of federal support, perhaps it is inevitable.

My question is this, how are the science institutions prepared to cope with the politicization that will occur, the public scrutiny and debate that science issues will now be confronted with, the practical needs for coalition building that political recognition implies, the application of discretionary resources to long term national policy goals, as well as the need for trade-offs? There are risks with this new recognition. How are universities in particular planning to address the institutional changes that this major league of political policy focus entails?

DR. RISEN: The answer is it is going to depend a lot on the

institutions. Some of them are in very good shape. Some are in very poor shape and do not even know the issue is there yet.

I think that how they respond in the nature of the characteristics of institutions that have common types of responses is going to determine how it plays into national policy.

If all of the large state universities, for example, respond in a certain way and private based universities respond another way and private colleges in still a third way and community colleges and city-based colleges still a fourth way, we will find national policy will follow those categories.

If it turns out that all of the construction turns out to occur in politically powerful states, it will follow the political power in the same way the public works projects and dams and river projects and virtually everything else does.

Some schools are well set up to handle this, to deal with it as organizations and associations. Some of them do not even know the problem is there yet.

DR. LANGENBERG: My brief answer to your question is, "poorly at first, but they will learn."

DR. BARKER: My answer would be there will be a variety of different responses for which we should thank God or whoever; that from that variety will emerge something which will work.

I come back to the point that was made. Universities tend to survive. We do need to look at the different kinds of responses somewhat in an experimental fashion; Carnegie-Mellon is doing a very good experiment. We will have to see whether its responses longer term are better than that being made by some of the other universities. They are all responding.

CHAPTER FIFTEEN
"Summary of NCAR 38"

Dr. Charles M. Schoman, Jr.
DAVID W. TAYLOR NAVAL SHIP RESEARCH AND DEVELOPMENT CENTER

I have reviewed the presentations of the last three days to obtain an image of what was said. This image is of a "nation at risk" with science and technology, scientists and engineers coming to the rescue. The questions are: will the Federal policies clear the way? will they arrive in time? will they be appreciated? and will the people cheer or jeer? In this summary, I'll first go through the national situation which was a main theme of the conference, then outline some United States national R&D policies, then go into a main thrust of the conference-industrial competitiveness, and end with some myths and some sobering thoughts.

What is our National Situation?

The United States has so long been the leader in productivity, it didn't believe or realize other nations could catch it. It emphasized other things: marketing, finance, and the balance sheet. Now the U.S. is no longer the leader in some areas of R&D, and there is some real industrial competition. It is urgent to apply science and technology to revitalize the economy and national defense. We need a whole new concept, a concept leading to production where computers and interdisciplinary studies are used, and also a change in the attitude of universities towards the manufacturing industry. Universities should not look down on industry. Students should be better trained to enter into industry.

The United States spends more on R&D than any other country, $100 billion this year. That's more than Great Britain, Germany, Japan, and France combined. IBM alone will spend $4 billion this year. Industry is spending more than the Federal government. We have the best basic research in the world, but we are not making use of it. Japan is using small high technology companies to quickly exploit technology. Much of this is U.S. technology.

The U.S. has been remarkable in having, since the early 1950's, basically the same R&D policies. However, there have been different interpretations and emphases which make it seem as if there has been a change. U.S. science and technology have entered the big leagues and have been brought into the political process. With much more interest in Congress, the dangers of "scientific porkbarrel" and the politicalization of science arise. The United States needs new synergism among government, industry, and the universities. The U.S. is spending a lot on science and is doing it is an effective way, but anything can be improved.

What are the U.S. Current Trends and National R&D Policies?

There certainly has been a changing attitude towards national security, a changing economic situation, and a change in the role of government in society. The main goals for research and development are to revitalize the economy and to strengthen defense. But this R&D must be excellent, relevant, and appropriate. Our policy trends include an increase in military R&D, the strategic defense initiative, a decrease in non-military R&D, a shift towards the hard sciences, an increase in basic research which has been recognized as a Federal responsibility, and a great concern for the transfer of technology overseas. The Office of Science and Technology Policy (OSTP) is now in place. However, we must deal with budget deficits and they must be controlled, therefore, the reemphasis on control of non-defense R&D and expenditures. The policy trends are simple, concise and clear but not new.

What is being done to aid R&D and to increaes industrial competitiveness?

Many things are being done. However, it is too early to tell exactly what the impact will be, but it is generally thought to be favorable. What has been done? Well, we have started to increase the quality of education at all levels, to increase funding for basic research in the universities, and provide incentives for R&D tax credits (these credits expire in three years). They should be continuing long term for their psychological effect on the chief executive officers of companies and the boards. Nothing is worse on the industrial decision process than uncertainty). We are also reducing regulatory restrictions; taking action to protect individual intellect, using the Federal labs and Federal dollars more effectively; stimulating R&D partnerships; seeking new methods of technology transfer to industry, placing more emphasis on manufacturing technology; establishing engineering centers; obtaining better sector interaction; recognizing the need to improve and modernize our university equipment instrumentation and facilities; reviewing the missions and roles of Federal labs. Recognizing that we must build technical talent in the U.S. (Ph.D. grants and math/science teacher awards are prime examples); placing special emphasis on biotechnology to agriculture; and recognizing that education, research and development go together. To this end, there have been 300 bills introduced in Congress and a number of bills have passed concerning R&D tax credits, the small business research act, math/science in elementary schools, cooperative R&D programs, patent term restoration, the National Science

Foundation charter amendments, manufacturing technology, and the robotics R&D act.

The Reagan administration impact can be clearly seen on funding for National R&D expenditures. Both Federal and non-Federal, have been going up. Academic non-Federal funding increased and after sort of a rocky start in 1982 and 1983, Federal funding is going up. Defense is increasing; non-defense varies but has decreased in energy and transportation where the appropriateness of the research has not been proven. Basic research-Federal and non-Federal is increasing; applied research-non-Federal is increasing and Federal decreasing. Development, both Federal and non-Federal, is increasing but industry is increasing the most.

Where does this all lead and why are we all doing all of this?

We are doing this to regain industrial competitiveness for the commercialization of technology. This is critical to our economic and social well being. This commercialization of technology involves research, development, production, marketing and sales, and it all starts with education. There must be synergism among the sectors, and in this synergism, it is hoped that something new will happen. To obtain this synergism, many research parks are starting, however, these must be well thought out and many will fail.

As we heard, research must be excellent, have relevance and be appropriate. These are the tests the Federal government is using. Our quality of research is really in good shape. The problem is we must use it to increase productivity, and in doing this it is not always something called high technology. Useful technology is what is necessary, useful to apply to the production process to increase productivity.

Industry is spending more on R&D and it is driving things. This is good and this has been forced by the Federal government. In design, we must use more computers, not only in design, but in manufacturing. We can do this as a result of the computer revolution. We must focus on the process of innovation, but also remember that many decisions are based on the health of the balance sheet. There is just so much capital in the capital pool and it is competed for to use in expansion and extension of business, to meet regulatory requirements such as pollution, and to develop new products and business. We must have capital to pursue new options, new processes, and to obtain new people. If we are not careful, the government policies will endanger the capital pool. A recent Presidential Commission on Industrial Competitiveness (PCIC) recommended (1) R&D partnerships, (2) industry funding of universities, (3) more manufacturing technology, (4) business schools emphasizing technology more, and

184

(5) engineering schools reemphasizing engineering.

When we talk about industrial competitiveness here in the United States, we generally think of large industry. We must not forget small business. Small business must be supported by the scientific establishment. In the U.S. there are some 14 million small businesses, each of which employs less than 500 people. These businesses have been frozen out by the rise of selective institutions. Most large universities are not interested in small business. However, the small business innovation research program has been a force in joining together universities, university professors and small business. This is generally an excellent program. However, the six months response time is costly to small business.

Universities and government can do a much better job for industry. Universities provide industry with knowledge and people, and the quality of people they are furnishing is high. There is also need for better scientific communications, a need within the universities. But we must be careful because in defense technology there is a security problem. There are also, we might add, industry proprietary items. Universities are the most stable institution that man has developed and they have been able to adjust to change. The new requirement of the Federal government will be the responsibility to upgrade the facilities of universities. This is a major problem and will take billions of dollars.

Myths?

Now, in looking over all that was said at the meeting, there are a number of myths or assumptions on which our whole system has been developed. These myths are: R&D describes a group of homogenous activities; R&D falls into nice categories: basic research, applied research and demonstration; basic research is the key to technological innovation; government puts in dollars and scientists establish priorities; government can't and shouldn't pick the winner; peer review is good for selecting projects; research and technology go together; and the level of spending is not a good level. These are some of the myths or assumptions on which we are developing our policies. The degree to which they are true or false, certainly has an impact on policy and its implementation.

One sobering thought that was brought up many times during the conference was that someday there will be an accounting. The politicians and the people will want to know what they got for the R&D dollars. We have to prepare for this day of reckoning.

(The author appreciates the aid given to him by many NCAR participants in preparing this summary, particularly J. Spates and W. Clearwaters who took extensive notes which were combined with the author's notes to develop this summary.)

CONCLUDING REMARKS

DR. HOGAN: The final comment and the concluding remarks will now be made by Cy Betts. Cy.

GENERAL BETTS: I thought that it might be useful to point out particularly what my good friend, Bill Frederick, indicated as the division of interests in this meeting.

The attendance score, as I last saw it, was 52 university representatives, 32 from industry, 33 from government, and 13 from the not-for-profits. That is not a precise division, but it gives you some idea of the distribution of interests.

I would remind you that next year, beginning the 29th of September, which is a Sunday, and running through the 2nd of October, we will have a meeting at the Keystone Resort, about 75 miles west of Denver, under the auspices of Denver Research Institute and that university.

In 1986 our meeting will be joint with the Canadian Research Management Association. And in 1987 we will violate our geographical pattern of attendance at meetings and accept Penn State's invitation to go back there for the 40th anniversary, which will actually be meeting number 41.

I do not have any other really important things to do except turn to gavel over to Dennis Barnes, who will be chair next year.

DR. BARNES: Thank you, Cy. As my first official act, I declare this conference adjourned.

MONDAY, OCTOBER 8, 1984

CONFERENCE ASSEMBLY

Opening Remarks -- A. W. Betts

Host Remarks -- Nanette Levinson

Host Welcome -- Richard Berendzen

Commonwealth Welcome -- Dennis W. Barnes

Program Introduction -- Thomas J. Hogan

Keynote Address -- Ian M. Ross

Quantitative S&T Overview -- Charles E. Falk

SESSION I - ADMINISTRATION POLICY

Session Chair -- John D. Holmfeld

Speaker -- James Ling

SESSION II - IMPACTS ON INDUSTRY

Session Chair -- Charles F. Larson

Speakers -- Milton D. Stewart
Samuel W. Tinsley
Mary L. Good

TUESDAY, OCTOBER 9, 1984

SESSION III -- IMPACTS ON THE GOVERNMENT

Session Chair -- Walter A. Hahn

Speakers -- Christopher T. Hill
Albert H. Teich

SESSION IV -- SMALL GROUP DISCUSSIONS

Session Chair -- George Gamota

WEDNESDAY, OCTOBER 10, 1984

SESSION V -- IMPACTS ON UNIVERSITIES

Session Chair -- Don I. Phillips

Speakers -- William R. Risen, Jr.
Robert Barker
Donald N. Langenberg

SESSION VI -- CONCLUDING DISCUSSION

Session Chair -- Charles M. Schoman, Jr.

CLOSING REMARKS -- A.W. Betts

FUTURE MEETINGS

NCAR 39

Keystone, Colorado
September 30 - October 2
Host: Shirley A. Johnson, Jr.
       Director, Denver Research Institute

NCAR 40

Quebec City, Canada
Joint Meeting with the
Canadian Research Management Association
September 1986

For informationion about meeting invitations, contact:

Chester McKee
National Research Council
2101 Constitution Ave., N.W.
Washington, D.C. 20418

For information about NCAR, contact:

Dr. Norman Waks, Executive Secretary, NCAR
The MITRE Corporation
Burlington Road
Bedford, MA 01730

NCAR 38 PARTICIPANTS

Tommy W. Ambrose
Battelle Memorial Institute

John M. Albertine
American Business Conferences

L. R. Ambrosini
U.S. Army

Carl B. Amthor
Associated Universities, Inc.

Robert C. Anderson
The University of Georgia

Donald L. Baeder
Occidental Chemical

H.W. Baldwin
The University of Western Ontario

Robert Barker
Cornell University

Robert C. Barlow
General Dynamics Corporation

Dennis Barnes
University of Virginia

Georges Bata
National Research Council Canada

Thomas Beaver, Jr.
The Pennsylvania State University

Ronald E. Becker

Edwin L. Behrens
Proctor and Gamble

Richard E. Berendzen
The American University

Austin W. Betts
Southwest Research Inst.

William R. Boyle
Oak Ridge Assoc. Universities

D. D. Browning
Armstrong World Industries, Inc.

James H. Burrows
National Bureau of Standards

Wayne G. Burwell
United Technologies Research Center

Kim Chaffee
Innotech Corporation

Bertrand Chatel
ISTAT, Inc. - INOVA

Cedric L. Chernick
Searle Scholars Program

Earl G. L. Cilley
Stanford University

Walter L. Clearwaters
Naval Underwater Systems Center

Robert E. Cleary
The American University

J. C. Clunie
West Point Pepperell

C. J. Cook
Bechtel Group, Inc.

Martin J. Cooper
Rohrback Technology

John C. Crowley
Association of American Universities

Harold L. Crutcher
Crutcher Consultant

Harold A. Daw
New Mexico State University

Nathan W. Dean
University of Georgia

Robert Eichelberger
Army Ballistic R&D Lab

Mark Elder
Arizona State University

Frederic H. Erbisch
Michigan Tech University

Robert N. Faiman
Air Force Inst. of Technology

Charles E. Falk
National Science Foundation

Robert C. Fitzpatrick
SUNY at Buffalo

William A. Frederick
Pennsylvania Power & Light Co.

Earl J. Freise
University of Nebraska - Lincoln

Norman W. Friedman
National Science Foundation

Osmund T. Fundingsland
U.S. General Accounting Office

George Gamota
The University of Michigan

Robert P. Glaze
Univ. of Alabama in Birmingham

Howard Gobstein
U.S. General Accounting Office

Milton Goldberg
Council on Governmental Relations

Mary L. Good
Signal UOP - Research Center

Kenneth F. Gordon
President's Commission on Industrial Competitiveness

Ann H. Greenberg
New York University

Laurel Grotzinger
Western Michigan University

Margaret Grucza
National Science Foundation

Peter Gwynne
MIT

Walter A. Hahn
George Washington University

Richard L. Haley
U.S. Army

John R. Hansen
TRW

Roger D. Hartman

R. W. Hennington
Clemson University

George R. Herbert
Research Triangle Inst.

Christopher T. Hill
Library of Congress

John C. Hockett
Governors State University

Thomas J. Hogan
National Science Foundation

George R. Holcomb
University of North Carolina

John D. Holmfeld
House Committee on Science and Technology

Gerald R. Hooper
VPI & SU

Shirley A. Johnson, Jr.
University of Denver

Jay T. Katz
The University of Michigan

V. Wayne Kennedy
University of California

Carlos Kruytbosch
National Science Foundation

Vincent R. Landi
Rogers Corporation

Donald N. Langenberg
University of Illinois at Chicago

Charles F. Larson
Industrial Research Inst.

Lorraine Lasker
New York Medical College

F. C. Leavitt
Dow Chemical USA

Nanette S. Levinson
The American University

J. M. Lewallen
Southwest Research Inst.

Gordon M. MacNabb
Natural Sciences & Engineering Research Council

James E. Mahoney
Department of Health & Human Services

Samuel A. Massenberg
NASA Langley Research Center

Stanley M. Matelski
The American University

Richard D. Mathieu
US Naval Academy

Marshall Mazer
Bethlehem Steel, Corporation

Willie L. McDaniel
Mississippi State University

Chester McKee
National Research Council

Herbert R. McLure
U.S. General Accounting Office

Richard P. McNitt

Anthony Merritt
University of Pennsylvania

Florence I. Metz
IIHS

Egils Milbergs
Department of Commerce

Frederick J. Milford
Battelle Columbus Labs

Gordon M. Monteath
Office of Naval Research

David D. Moran
David Taylor Naval Ship R&D Center

Stanley G. Nicholas
Clemson University

Julie T. Norris
University of Houston

C. J. Nyman
Washington State University

George A. Paulikas
The Aerospace Corporation

Heinz G. Pfeiffer
Pennsylvania Power & Light Co.

Don I. Phillips
Government-University-Industry Research Ro

James S. Pierce
Bureau of Reclamation

Ralph E. Powe
Mississippi State University

Samuel F. Powel III
U.S. Coast Guard R&D Center

Edward J. Poziomek
Chemical Research & Development Center

Richard E. Quinn
RCA Laboratories

Forrest J. Remick
Penn State University

William R. Richard
Monsanto Industrial Chemicals

William M. Risen, Jr.
Brown University

Debra Rogers
Digital Equipment Corporation

Ian M. Ross
AT&T-Bell Laboratories

Sidney Ross
RCA

Eric R. Rude
University of Wisconsin at Madison

Charles M. Schoman
David Taylor Naval Ship Research & Development Center

E. P. Senger, Jr.
Memphis State University

Jill Smith
Army Ballistics R&D Lab

Howard E. Sorrows
National Bureau of Standards

James Spates
Department of the Army

D. C. Spriestersbach
The University of Iowa

James R. Stevenson
Georgia Institute of Technology

Milton D. Stewart
Robbins & Greene

Delia Stoehr
Naval Research Laboratory

Albert H. Teich
AAAS

Samuel M. Tennant
Aerospace Corporation

John H. Thompson
University of Pittsburg

Samuel W. Tinsley
Union Carbide Corporation

William E. Tossell
University of Guelph

Jack R. Van Lopik
Louisiana State University

Norman Waks
The Mitre Corporation

Eric A. Walker
Penn State University

Janet Wall
Naval Postgraduate School

Cormac P. Walsh
Eagle Research Group, Inc.

Donald Waterman
University of Houston

Barbara D. Webster
University of California

Robert E. Weigle
US Army Research Office

W. Bruce Wheaton
University of Iowa

M. Kent Wilson
National Science Foundation

Franklin E. Wolf, Jr.
NTEC

William E. Woolam
Southwest Research Institute

James J. Worth
BioAssay Systems Corp.

John C. Wurst
University of Dayton

Leo Young
ODUSDRE (R&AT/RLM)

Daniel J. Zaffarano
Iowa State University

Kenton W. Zahrt
Planning Consultant

APPENDIX FOUR
THE NATIONAL CONFERENCE ON
THE ADVANCEMENT OF RESEARCH

The growth of research and development (R&D) since World War II has confronted leaders in the R&D infrastructure of our country with the need to develop and articulate national policies and management practices appropriate to the role of science, engineering and technology as major factors in the well-being and health of the nation.

For nearly four decades the National Conference on the Advancement of Research (NCAR), has contributed to satisfying this need by providing a forum at which senior managers of R&D can study issues and exchange views, particularly as they relate to the interactions among the four sectors: government, industry, universities, and R&D and related professional service organizations.

NCAR PAST AND PRESENT

The first NCAR meeting, under the name of National Conference on the Administration of Research, was held at Pennsylvania State College in 1947. It was attended by 171 scientists and administrators who had been actively engaged in the management of our R&D effort during World War II.

The Conference has continued from year to year since that time, and has developed a character based upon four main features: informality, talks by eminent speakers, interactive discussions (including small seminars), and balanced representation from the four R&D sectors.

Recent meetings have explored as themes new thrusts and directions in R&D, the need to modify these thrusts in changing times, the search for innovative solutions to national problems, and the new challenges of increasing demands on limited resources. Reflecting this growing interest in broader issues, the name was changed in 1974 by substituting "Advancement" for "Administration."

NCAR meetings are held for three days each autumn in different parts of the country. One afternoon is kept open for informal association.

Each conference is managed by a host institution which changes each year, usually a university. The host makes arrangements for the site and facilities, issues the invitations, and manages all physical and financial matters. There are no dues, but conferees pay a nominal conference fee to defray expenses of the meeting.

Invitations are extended to individuals on the basis of their experience and accomplishments in the management and direction of R&D, their potential contribution to the discussions, and the desire for interaction among a broad range of disciplines from all four sectors. Suggestions concerning qualified participants to be added to the list of invitees are welcomed.

CONFERENCE COMMITTEE

Overall responsibility for NCAR rests with a conference committee of approximately 29 members. Working through sub-committees as appropriate, the committee selects and approves host institutions and dates for future conferences, appoints the conference and program chairmen, develops the invitation list, reviews the budget submitted by the host, and sets policies and directions for the conduct of the conference. New members are elected by the committee for four year terms as vacancies occur, maintaining balanced representation from the four sectors. In addition, the membership includes an Executive Secretary, who provides a corporate memory for NCAR.

NAME LIST